Colloquium: Sound Art and Music

Colloquium: Sound Art and Music

Edited by Thomas Gardner

and Salomé Voegelin

zero books

Winchester, UK
Washington, USA

First published by Zero Books, 2016
Zero Books is an imprint of John Hunt Publishing Ltd., Laurel House, Station Approach,
Alresford, Hants, SO24 9JH, UK
office1@jhpbooks.net
www.johnhuntpublishing.com
www.zero-books.net

For distributor details and how to order please visit the 'Ordering' section on our website.

ISBN: 978 1 78279 895 8
Library of Congress Control Number: 2015960679

A CIP catalogue record for this book is available from the British Library.

Design: Stuart Davies

CONTENTS

Acknowledgements

We want to thank the London College of Communication, University of the Arts London, who kindly supported the Colloquium that inspired and informed this publication. We also want to thank the technical team, Ciaran Harte, Paul Richardson and MA Sound Arts Alumni, who have arranged the recordings of the day, and all the participants who joined us for a day of discussion on a theme we believe holds much current import and poses many questions for the future of both sound art and music.

Preface

In October 2012, Thomas Gardner and Salomé Voegelin hosted a colloquium, entitled Sound Art and Music: historical continuum and mimetic fissures[1], at the London College of Communication, University of the Arts London. This colloquium dealt with a current debate concerning the relationship between sound art and music and focused on the precept that sound art and music evolve in a shared world and that the joint navigation of this common terrain would allow for new creative approaches to be taken and new critical insights to be established on how we produce, listen to and engage in works with sound.

This colloquium was motivated by the lack of a joint critical framework for sound art and music and was inspired by their persistent separation: the politics of their disciplinary boundaries; the aesthetic expectations that maintain them, tradition, economics and education; as well as the practicalities of their transgression. It framed a discussion, critique and debate around the relationship between sound art and music from different vantage points: exploring aesthetic, commercial, technological, as well as emotional and ritualistic reasons to keep them separate or to build a continuum within their practice and theorisation. The main objective was to ignite a discourse between sound art and music, to provoke and propose languages and strategies that would enable artists, musicians, curators and scholars as well as a general audience to negotiate joint listening in this territory.

The invited participants were: Simon Emmerson, Allen S. Weiss, Cathy Lane, Volkmar Klien, Leigh Landy, Claudia Molitor, Aura Satz, Angus Carlyle, Nye Parry, John Wynne, Peter Cusack, John Drever, Robert Worby, Michael Young, Anna Gritz, David Toop, Kathy Hinde, Seth Ayyez, Stephen Preston, Ed Baxter, Justin Yang, Helen Frosi, Max Eastley, and Salomé Voegelin and Thomas Gardner. They all agreed to spend a day together, debating the possibilities and significance of sound art's association with music.

This book proposes to open the closed colloquium setting to a wider audience through the publication of a decisive range of the material that defined the event. This includes the pre-prepared provocations that initiated the three parts of the colloquium; the transcriptions of the debates as they ensued on the day, documenting the challenging, rich, and at times argumentative discussion that ensued; and the responses produced after the event to reflect on the transcribed material and to elaborate on specific points raised during the discussions. This three-part structure is postscripted with an essay by Kate Lacey. Working as an outsider, not identifying herself as a musician or sound artist, and not present on the day, she observes the proceedings and engages with their content in a current reflection.

The aims of this book are to initiate a debate about the relationship between sound art and music, to raise some pressing and relevant issues about this relationship without necessarily providing answers, and to open the field for discussions that will entice a professional audience as well as a broader public to engage in listening between the concert hall and the gallery space, between the record collection, the radio and online listening, and the site of an installation or the expectation of the exhibition format.

The book's organisation follows the three themed sessions that took place on the day. Each session is represented here by two provocations, followed by the ensuing transcribed discussions, followed by two written responses. The provocations and responses frame the transcripts, drawing out the significance of the live engagement and offering the reader further points of contact. The transcripts aim to give insight into the areas covered and the language employed, to reveal the rhythms that unfold between provocations, discussions and responses. The subsections were named after the event, their titles teasing out and highlighting the central themes that emerged from the discussions, which were further pursued in the responses that took the form of essays, conversations, interviews and work reports. The variety of formats reflect the different backgrounds and perspectives of the participants and express the plurality of views on whether and how sound art and music meet in practice, in discourse and in listening.

Notes

1 This title was subsequently given to a special issue of *Organised Sound* (20/2, August 2015, Cambridge University Press), edited jointly by Thomas Gardner and Salomé Voegelin, with contributions solicited through an open call inviting artists, curators, theorists, writers, and listeners to discuss the relationship between sound art and music. The journal issue presents an additional incarnation and strategy in the debate around the continuum or fissure between sound art and music, which this book tries to develop. The journal too was facilitated by the initial colloquium discussions and in its own way opened a broader participation through a peer-reviewed reworking. http://journals.cambridge.org action/displayJournal?jid=OSO

PART ONE:
Tradition, Codification, and Materiality

Provocations

Abstracts

Allen S. Weiss

The 20th century has seen music at the centre of a continuing polemic about its forms and limits: tonal vs atonal, music vs noise, high vs low, and now music vs sound art. In fact, our modalities of listening as well as the use-value of sounds are in constant transformation, and the above dichotomies reveal the richness of organised sound. According to historical circumstances, one and the same sound can be transformed from noise to mystery to imitation of nature to imitation of music to music. A fascinating case in point is the *suikinkutsu* (literally 'water zither cave'), a Japanese instrument created in the early Edo period: a sort of pot buried underneath the laver where one ritually purifies oneself before the tea ceremony, such that the water overflowing the laver enters the chamber and drips into a pool, creating sounds akin to that of the kin, a sort of Japanese zither. Originally, the mysterious presence of these sounds emanating from the earth would have served as a prelude to the highly codified sounds of the tea ceremony. But the confluence of modern noise pollution, the advent of non-traditional instruments, and the conception of the soundscape have annulled the mystery of these sounds and made of the *suikinkutsu* a new form of instrument.

Salomé Voegelin

At present traditional musical composition (which can be brought together under the terms contemporary classical, new classical or art music) and a contemporary sonic output (summarised in the term sound art) represent distinctly different practices and are approached through separate critical languages. While contemporary classical music is investigated via traditional musicology, most other sonic works are theorised in relation to visual arts discourse. Even as this visual affiliation has aided sound art's recognition, making it more visible, it has hidden its musical heritage and those aspects of its practice that recall that history. Consequently contemporary sonic output is rarely appreciated and approached as a critical response to previous and concurrent musical works but is mostly considered in relation to the concerns of visual practice and theory. In this opening statement I will articulate my desire for a comparative framework for sound art and traditional music that seeks not to simply affiliate sound art to music but aims to open music, musicology, its funding networks and performance platforms to sound art. What I want to put forward for discussion is the notion of a 'continuum of sound': to reconnect sound art with traditional music and to produce an analytical framework that can access and investigate both within one critical language.

First Provocation – Allen S. Weiss

The Limits of Representation: a case study of transformations in the sonic aesthetics of the Japanese tea ceremony[1]

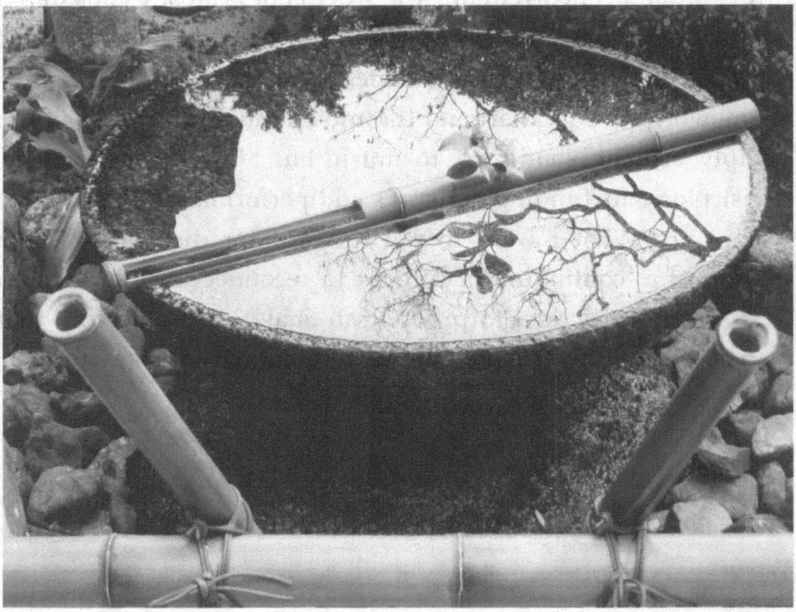

Suikinkutsu at Enkō-ji temple, Kyoto (Photo: Allen S. Weiss)

One of the most beautiful, though relatively unknown, types of Japanese sonic installations is the *suikinkutsu* (water zither cave), said to have been invented by the great tea master Kobori Enshū (1579–1647). The water that is used to purify the hands and mouth before the tea ceremony overflows from the *chōzubachi* (laver) into the *tsukubai* (the stone arrangement in which the laver is placed), and is then evacuated into the *suikinkutsu* (a small buried jar or chamber) where the water drips into a pool at the bottom, creating sounds akin to those of the kin, a type of zither.

As the guests kneel down in a gesture of ablution, they are met with a mysterious aquatic sound emanating from the earth. The *suikinkutsu* is usually made of pottery, with an irregular unglazed surface that causes numerous droplets of water to form and drip in irregular patterns, thus creating a complex sonic environment which we would now characterise in stochastic terms, where the earth resonates with the song of water. This aleatory 'music', as if of liquified earth, variously serves as purification of body and soul, as an anticipation of the pleasures of the tea ceremony, and as a prefiguration of the rare sounds that punctuate the stillness of the tea hut during the tea ceremony (*cha-no-yu*): hot water for tea. And yet this sound can not be named, situated or classified.

As it takes approximately twenty years to begin to master the tea ceremony, and here we have but a few minutes to grasp its essence, I would like to suggest its ambiance and synthesise its aesthetic with the help of several short lists. To harmonise the terms of these lists would be to imagine the proper mind-set required to appreciate tea aesthetics, stressing the role of the *roji* (dewy path) and the tea room as a site of extreme aesthetic concentration that functions in various parameters, each of which establishes a precise and codified set of sonic expectations, notably: the performance of the choreography of tea; the exhibition of objects in the *tokonoma* (alcove); the critical and ritualised examination and discussion of the art objects.

(1) The 'three sounds of tea': the clink of the lid on the kettle; the tap of the tea bowl on the mat; the clink of the tea spoon on the tea bowl: metal on metal, pottery on straw, wood on pottery – a sonic combinatory of the materials intrinsic to tea. But there is yet another sound, metaphoric and metonymic, one which links inside to outside, microcosm to macrocosm: the strains of the boiling kettle, which is said to sound like the wind in the

pines, not coincidentally, what is heard in one of the most famous traditional works for *shakuhachi* flute, *Matsukaze*. The novelist Kawabata Yasunari describes this effect in a scene from *Snow Country*: 'The innkeeper had lent him an old Kyoto teakettle, skilfully inlaid in silver with flowers and birds, and from it came the sound of wind in the pines. He could make out two pine breezes, as a matter of fact, a near one and a far one. Just beyond the far breeze he heard faintly the tinkling of a bell.' Thus the tea ceremony establishes a codified set of sonic expectations, in this case of water heard as wind.

(2) The four basic precepts of tea: harmony, respect, purity, tranquillity (*wa kei sei jaku*). A mix of Confucianism, Taoism, Shinto, Buddhism.

(3) Three forms of beauty (according to Haga Kōshirō): simple and unpretentious, imperfect and irregular, austere and stark.

(4) Four pertinent aesthetic features (according to Donald Keene): suggestion, irregularity, simplicity, perishability.

(5) Seven characteristics particular to the Zen sensibility (according to Hisamatsu Shin'ichi): asymmetry, simplicity, austere sublimity or lofty dryness, naturalness, subtle profundity or deep reserve, freedom from attachment, tranquillity.

(6) Aesthetic principles of *wabi* / *sabi* / *shibui*.

(a) *Wabi*: poverty, quietness, tranquillity, solitude, humbleness, frugality, unobtrusiveness, asymmetrical harmony, elegant rusticity.

(b) *Sabi*: literally rust; wear and patination by age and use; *sabi* denotes a sense of familiarity, continuity, history, antiquity, and a corresponding feeling of passing and loss, loneliness and melancholy; by extrapolation, in its extreme instances, it evokes bleakness, chilliness, desiccation, desolation, extinction.

(c) *Shibui*: literally 'astringent'; understatement, suggestion, restraint, modesty, discrimination, formality, serenity, quiet taste, refined simplicity, noble austerity.

To synthesise all of the above, impossible as it may be, would be to establish the mindset in which one could listen to the sound of the *suikinkutsu* in the context of a 17th-century tea ceremony. The most famous *suikinkutsu* extant is to be found in the Enkō-ji temple in Kyoto. However, the changes wrought by modernisation – vastly increased ambient noise and intensive tourism – have resulted in a radical transformation of the social and symbolic functions of this instrument, as well as changes in its form.

In a monumental paradigm shift, the foundational aesthetic Zen discourse has given way to modernist Western modes of listening, in the epoch where, ironically, the democratisation of the tea ceremony has made its form available to everybody, but its depth all the more hidden. This new form of listening, according to which such sounds could be heard as music, needs to be considered according to both Western and Japanese musical genealogies, for example: Henry Cowell, *Aeolian Harp* (1923); Henry Cowell, *The Banshee* (1925); Edgar Varèse, *Ionisation* (1931); Pierre Schaeffer, *Études aux chemins de fer* (1948); John Cage, *4′33″* (1952); Olivier Messiaen, *Le merle bleu* (1956–58); Iannis Xenakis, *Concrète PH* (1958); Takemitsu Toru, *Water Music* (1960). With these sonic innovations in mind, we may now imagine the sounds of the *suikinkutsu* in both the context of a traditional tea ceremony and that of modernist music, as in Steve Feld's *Suikinkutsu* (2006), which begins with the raw recording of the *suikinkutsu* of Enkō-ji (Kyoto) with the ambient sound of cicadas, followed by a Cage-inspired mix of these very same sounds.

No longer do the sounds of this *suikinkutsu* offer an occult surprise for the privileged few chosen to attend a tea ceremony, since for the vast majority of attendees – who are now tourists – it has been turned into the mere curiosity of an unusual musical instrument. The secret, symbolic, esoteric sounds previously linked to the tea ceremony have been transmogrified into a public sonic event, a new form of music. This change is instantiated by the revised form of the instrument: previously, the entirety of the *suikinkutsu* was buried underground creating an invisibility that led to astonishment; but now wooden bamboo tubes have been inserted into the echo chamber to amplify and transmit the sound, so as to countervene the noisy ambiance. Ironically, this tube system also serves as a barrier, so that the laver cannot be approached and utilised, effectively transforming the *suikinkutsu* into a sculpture, a situation reinforced by the fact that the ladle that normally would be laid across the bamboo support spanning the *chōzubachi* is now usually absent. The *suikinkutsu* thus loses its surprise effect just as the *chōzubachi* is deprived of its purifying function. It is no longer the gesture of purification that creates the sound, but rather the water's constant flow, without human intervention. We experience modern music of a sort, not the poetic resonance of the tea ceremony as a performance of purification.

Notes

1 This text is based on a section of Allen S. Weiss, *Zen Landscapes: Perspectives on Japanese Gardens and Ceramics* (Reaktion Books, 2013).

Second Provocation – Salomé Voegelin

Historical Interest: a pragmatic provocation for a continuum of sound

My short statement that was sent out to you with the invitation to this colloquium, and that is represented here by the abstract, articulates my desire to reconnect sound art with music and to produce an analytical framework that can access and investigate both within one theoretical context. What I want to put forward for discussion is the notion of a 'continuum of sound' understood not as an unproblematic, homogenous line of attribution and reference, but as a complex, contradictory, even antagonistic field within which a comparative study of all that sounds can take place.

In the background of this desire for a comparative study of sonic works across genres and times is my sense that there is something we do not hear in contemporary musical and sound art works because our perception is at once enabled and limited by disciplinary frameworks, pedagogic schemes, habits, and expectations, rather than through an open and pluralistic listening. I am persuaded that there is the potential for a different listening, hearing, and theorisation that we cannot achieve because, hindered by 'disciplinary correctness', we lack a joint critical framework to analyse, study, and interpret traditional musical composition and a contemporary sonic output. I believe that there is something we cannot hear, that remains inaudible in the works we listen to if we do not hear them within the holistic and plural complexity of influences and histories, and if instead we seek to explain and explore them within separate frameworks and in relation to non-sounding paradigms.

I will try to briefly clarify what I mean and take 1950 as a not entirely accurate but not entirely arbitrary date either: at that point some sonic expressions left the classical musical trajectory and under the term electroacoustic composition built their own context, still as music, but to the side of what was going on in conservatoires. Then, in and around the 1960s and 1970s, other musicians developed soundscape compositions and soundscape research that have found a context within and without musical theorisation towards anthropology, social geography, and social studies. Most other sonic work that does not play within those two groups, and yet also does not conform to conservatory expectations, has found a home, through the legacy of Fluxus, within the context of visual arts. (I am aware that I am leaving radio art to one side here for now.)

While this visual arts context has given sound art visibility and popularity it has not necessarily made it more audible. In fact I would argue that the heavy contextual and conceptual focus of contemporary visual art's discourse has impeded the development of a critical listening practice that could make accessible, audible, and thinkable the sound in the work. The visual discourse does not invite listening as a generative practice or as exploration of the work's materiality. Consequently sonic works in the visual art's context are mainly talked about for what they look like and what concepts they represent rather than what they sound like and thus what concepts they produce. They are rarely considered for their sonic materiality or understood to be produced through an auditory experience, but for meanings and concepts that are staged and signalled but not realised in sound, and that are at best illustrative of but never produced or explored through its material.

Some may think this is a small price to pay for visibility and popularity and are happy to work on visual terrain, but I think the price is far too high and indeed that it is not only sound art but visual art itself that is missing a chance to invigorate its flat conceptuality with the demanding materiality of sound.

On this background and for this reason, I want to claim some of music's heritage for sound art. I want to lay claim to music's history as one of sound art's histories, and propose that considering sound art in relation to music can bring about a new focus on sound in art: on its materiality *and* its conceptuality, on how we produce and how we participate in works, and on the demand of the invisible, which challenges and augments what we see, and can help us access what remains inaudible within other contexts too. This is, importantly, not a laying-claim to music theory and musicology's history, but to the history of musical practice, its processes and outcomes, as an important provenance of sound art that in turn it gives its future.

This musical heritage, I believe, would enable a theorisation of works with sound from listening rather than through ideas of concept, structure and context alone: from the material as it were rather than from ideas. In this way it would reveal and disregard the limitations of the conceptual and contextual focus of visual discourse, and it would also contest a musicological attention on the score, on biography and more recently on context, implode its traditional frame of reference, and allow us to listen to music as a listening to sound, to write about it from the heard rather than from the infrastructure of its theorisation. From there music and sound art could share a plural listening, offering a comparative field that could purview visual arts too.

By claiming music's heritage for sound art I do not mean to plot a homogenous line or to make an orderly historical chronology, and neither do I want to use a conventional musicology or music theory to explore and identify contemporary sonic works. Rather, I believe that my re-affiliation of sound work with music has the more radical consequence of not only reconsidering and augmenting how we talk about sound arts, what references we pursue, and what histories we construct, but that it will also radicalise the classic musical paradigm: challenging its aesthetic, theoretical, educational as well as its financial homogeneity and hegemony.

Music theory and musicology and conservatoire teaching has had quite an easy time of it for the last sixty years or so: everybody and anything that could have disrupted its aesthetic and historical conventions and canons has moved sideways and left its frame of reference, or has acquired a prefix that clears it out of the way of the original stem: ethno-, socio-, feminist-, etc. There are very few radicalisms to be found within the base term of (new) classical music; very few challenges have managed to disturb classical ears. I want to confront those ears to make them hear sound, and at the same time bring what is central to musical practice – its focus on materiality, sentiment, emotions and participation, all issues eschewed in visual arts discourse – to bear on sound art.

There are many reasons why I want part of this heritage, why I think it is due to sound art, and why I believe it is necessary we pursue it. Some of those are very pragmatic:

I want the funding, the sponsorship and the publicity that is granted classical music to benefit a broader sonic expression. Thus I want the concert halls, the opera houses, as spaces where sound art can be performed and installed, not necessarily instead of but together with music, so that sound art might confront the expectations set up by its buildings and conventions, to invite different auditions that expand traditional significance and value.

I want school pupils to be taught about post-serial sonic explorations, and by that I do not mean the Beatles and pop songs or folk, but the broad spectrum of sonic works that have been produced for well over a century now. I believe they need to hear a plurality of sounds in order to gain an understanding of its materiality, its concepts and artistic possibilities that are not inaccessible and inarticulate per se but are made to appear so by a current theorisation and valuation; and they need to hear that sound in relation to classical music, not as a controversial act against music, nor as an element of visual arts only.

I want a contemporary audience to be able to listen to contemporary sonic works and have some strategies and ideas about how to engage with them so they do not avoid the sonic in favour of its visual frame, be that the score, the words of the vocalists, the installation setup or the catalogue text. I want to invite them to listen to the work in relation to historical and contemporary references, musical and artistic, however burdened and complex they might seem, to make them hear the differences and similarities as a matter of artistic intention and significance, rather than simply keep them separate in a visual indifference to such material relationships. I believe it serves us all to appreciate and participate in sound's invisible possibilities that might make us see things in new ways.

Other reasons to insist on this (classical) musical heritage for sound art are aesthetic and even ideological:

I want the craft aspect of classical music, the indulgence in materiality, and its jouissance brought to bare on the criticism and theorisation of sonic works, any works with sound, so that their own jouissance does not wither away in a conceptual and contextual environment of visual arts where emotions, sentiment, joy, and pleasure are mostly theorised away or understood as concepts rather than felt.

I want to be able to compare works such as Henry Purcells' *March for the Funeral of Queen Mary* with Janet Cardiff and George Bures Miller's *Deep Pool* sound installation, and Alban Berg's Opera *Woyzeck* with Doug Aitken's piece *Frontier*, to perform a comparative study of how to listen to them in a way that does not focus on the themes and concepts, and not on harmony and musical language either, but that focuses on the experience of the work as a spatiotemporal environment generated in sound. I believe it is there, in a listening free of music-theoretical limitations and not bound to visual concepts, that comparisons across genres and times can become possible and that music comes to be an environment that we inhabit through listening; an environment that is made up of music and sound simultaneously, and thus a critical comparison between the two becomes a possibility.

Then any work with sound becomes a sound work becomes sound art. The continuum between music and sound art is the formless form of their relationship that does not prevent antagonism and contradiction but enables a shared listening and a comparative theorisation that can make the inaudible heard and new things seen.

As an endnote, and to clarify: the term music in this context refers to classical, new classical, or art music, which I position and identify as a cultural equivalent of visual arts. An argument could be made that the continuum I am promoting here should include folk, pop, world music, and indeed any form of music. While I understand the principle of this request, I am for now and in this provocation remaining with this comparative focus due to the financial, ideological, and aesthetic issues and investments that I see to be shared by visual art and (new) classical music. No doubt other relationships might be argued for between pop, folk, world music, and sound art, but those would by necessity have to involve a discussion of the very different theoretical and curatorial infrastructure and circumstance of these practices.

Transcript of First Colloquium Discussion

Stephen Preston: Thinking of the democratisation of the *suikinkutsu*, it sounds as if the tea ceremony becomes empty of content, it's no longer listening, it's only hearing. [...]

Allen S. Weiss: I think you're probably right about this democratisation emptying out the mystical content from the tea ceremony, and a certain mystery from the sound of the *suikinkutsu*, but what it also does is open up an indefinite number of other possibilities of listening. That's precisely why I played the beginning of Takemitsu's *Water Music*. [...] The reason that becomes interesting is because of the extraordinarily high degree of codification in Japanese aesthetics, even to this day. What the electroacoustic set of possibilities does (Takemitsu's electroacoustic piece was a relatively early one, 1960) is create another set of opportunities which then make sense within a millennium-and-a-half old set of symbolic codifications. [...]

Justin Yang: I want to respond to what Allen was saying. I've been giving a lot of thought to content-driven listening. In particular I have been thinking about recorded and improvised music. Listening to the Coltrane record *Interstellar Space* I couldn't hum it, however I have a really distinct experience of 'in the moment' listening because of the nature of the material. I think it does translate into recorded music, whereas listening to Glenn Gould playing Brahms' *Intermezzi* is a different mode of listening, based on content. [...] So I'm wondering if, in your particular example, the context cannot be reflected in the actual document, in the recorded music itself.

Allen: I could answer directly. I'll begin with the Coltrane. I was involved in the music and I listened to a lot of recorded jazz. At one point I was able to scat-sing the entirety of Afro Blues [laughter]. So this is something that recording does. It's a silly anecdote, but you can look at it historically. For example, in the first recording of Charlie Parker and Lester Young together (Charlie Parker learned many of his riffs by listening to Lester Young records), in the third tune everyone walked offstage, he blew them away – everyone walked off stage, including Lester Young. [...] The point being that all these people are improvising on the basis of repetition, of recorded music that itself wasn't written down, and in traditional Japanese aesthetics, even today, what happens is very highly codified. In traditional Japanese poetry if you mention 'the river' what it means is the Kamo River in Kyoto. So in fact, as both of you were saying, it is content-driven. It is content- and subject-driven to the point of creating extraordinary constraints, and it is within those constraints that one, as it were, improvises and comes up with new combinations or new poetry.

Justin: [...] I'll name another piece, Christian Wolff's *Long Piano*, it was the same sort of experience. I can't identify any of the material, but I definitely had the experience of being completely 'in the moment' because of the nature of the material, and then forgetting about it. The New York School did that very well. Feldman and Cage had this in common, even though the music is stylistically so different. They had this sense of bringing you into the moment, and I think it does translate to recording. I'm not sure, but I think it does, whereas if I listen to the Brahms—

Volkmar Klien: But if I could come back to Salomé. Wouldn't listening to music as sound simply be not hearing music? As a parallel, if you listen to language as sound you just don't 'get it' (you don't get what is being said), and it's impossible for the human brain to do so. There is a psychoacoustic experiment which reduces a voice to four or five sine tones; the first couple of seconds you hear sound, and then your brain realises 'I can understand it' and it goes 'click' and you understand what's being said, and there's no way of finding your way back. Of course this is only proven in terms of psychoacoustics for language, but I think there is a parallel to music, that music isn't just sound and its not just organised sound either, for language is organised sound too and is not music.

Salomé: But I'd like to turn that around then. Because if I switch on some Brahms, because it was just mentioned, and I say 'I'm listening to music', I don't hear anything else. And that's a problem too because then I can only hear what pertains within that piece to the musical language. What I am suggesting, and of course this is a provocation and I wouldn't turn everything around 100% and eradicate music, is that a) it remains its own category and has all these problems of hegemony and scholarship and sponsorship et cetera, and b) we can't hear anything else. There is something that's inaudible and that remains inaudible. I'm quite glad that you mentioned Morton Feldman because with Feldman you hear something in the moment. I kind of acknowledge it as music, I acknowledge it as a musical context, as a musical environment, but if I would strip it down to the musical language I would miss what it is in the moment, which then maybe I can't hum afterwards and which I can't go and write down afterwards but which I retain in my body as a physical inhabited experience. My issue with musical listening and music education (of course it is again very personal how you've received your own music education) is that you look at the score, you look at the partitur, you learn it and you know what it does. Of course that is a reduction and there is a lot else that can be had. I do feel that we have reduced our culture by saying that the last sixty or so years of what's going on with sounds does not go in the great big concert halls and opera houses, has not got that sort of status, and isn't considered worth listening to.

Nye Parry: Boulez wanted to blow up the opera houses fifty years ago and they haven't been blown up yet.

Volkmar: He's quite happily conducting in them [laughter].

Nye: Well, he is quite happily conducting in them now, but maybe that's because he lost the battle, I don't know.

Robert Worby: He also said he was a Leninist.

Simon Emmerson: Can I say we are skirting around an absolutely fundamental thing. I have a sort of Garden of Eden view of an infinite mythical past: we've rent asunder three things, and the third one has been mentioned without being made explicit. The content, the listening strategy, and thirdly the environment in which it's being listened to, which has two dimensions, a physical one and a sociological one. An opera house is not just a building, clearly it's a social construction, and listening to Takemitsu now is a different listening mode from being in a concert hall listening to Takemitsu, just as listening to Lester Young live would clearly be different from listening to recordings. It's absolutely vital that these three, if we can't put them back together again, be at least brought into some relationship. What I like about Salomé's subversive point, and Nye's response to it, is that it is precisely in the rubbing together of the impossibility of thinking of an opera house—

Volkmar: The opera house is not going to die [laughter].

Nye: I think there is a deeper issue about institutions. I think you [Salomé] are offering a very institutional model, actually, of your definition of what belongs to music and how we listen to music, and what belongs to art and how we think of sound art in terms of art. You've got to remember that the conservatoires have agendas, which is your point to an extent, but those agendas colour what goes on there. If we think about Britain there are actually only about eight conservatoires, and are we really worried about what goes on in those eight conservatoires? I am, because I teach in two of them and what I teach is listening, and all the things that you would like to have happen in the conservatoire. Listening to the sound example you played at the end there, I could imagine a lot of my students producing that in the conservatoires. So I don't think that what happens within the institutions is such a problem. On the other hand I think the conservatoires do have a sense of themselves. You might be thinking about music departments in universities, and that's a very different thing because as we can see represented round the table there are a lot of very open minds in those places. But I think the conservatoire exists to legitimise a certain tradition and to keep the tradition alive, and it's a tradition that is under threat. So I think that what happens within the composition departments in conservatoires is always rubbing against what the rest of the conservatoire is about. You can see that in the struggle that student composers have getting people to play their pieces, even within the conservatoire. So I think that complex political issues colour the perceptions that you're talking about, and I think you are wanting to get to something that's much more about 'Do we treat music as a set of symbols?' and 'Do we reduce our listening?' I don't think that, outside of the conservatoire, people going to the Proms or going to a Mahler symphony do reduce in their minds the music they are listening to the score. The score is a representation that is backed up with a tradition of performance that brings back the aural into that music, and that is what's experienced by the listeners. Now, the more educated listeners will appreciate formal structures and musicological things and the fact that there are added ninths and things, whereas the less educated listeners will probably listen more in the moment, more phenomenologically, and have that kind of bathing in the sound experience.

Salomé: But I think that they will listen in the familiarity that the notion of the score gives, and with the continuity that that development of written-down music gives; what it makes possible and what it leaves as impossible.

Nye: You could look at familiarity as language acquisition.

Salomé: But that's what I'm saying. All that I want is that people learn other things, and I think that sound art is that other thing that just sort of conveniently went to one side and now remains often unheard within the visual arts.

Nye: Yeah, that's our problem and that, I think, is what we should be focusing on because that's the problem of the sound art community, it's not the problem of the classical-music world.

Aura Satz: I just wanted to bring the discussion round to address what Simon mentioned, in terms of the mode of listening. I find that really interesting, more so than the institutional conflicts. This idea of a mode of listening and a demanding materiality of the sound. I make films that are with sound and I wonder, [to Salomé] are you saying 'blindfold yourself' when you see the Doug Aitken piece that you played? I've seen the film of that, but I don't know which version you're referring to. So am I then expected to remove any visual reference? Is that what you're suggesting, or is it a mode of listening that can actually be applied to the visual world as well, so that it's a mode of listening that is a mode of paying attention, rather than something specifically related to the auditory?

Salomé: Absolutely, I think you can even listen to the visual. It is a certain sonic sensibility, where you give it time, where you engage with the demands of a sonic materiality. I think this is very often lost in visual arts discourse, which is concept- and context-heavy, rather than an indulgence in what happens to me while being in an installation of an artist like Doug Aitken (it's the installation in Rome). So there is a whole visual spectacle going on. But I didn't want to distract by showing visuals.

Aura: But that's the point. I feel that you're talking about the visual as a distraction or a movement away from paying attention. Whereas my Utopian version of paying attention, which is parallel to yours but perhaps slightly broader in terms of medium-specificity, is not that the visual is detracting or distracting or taking away from this attention to a demanding materiality, but rather I'm negotiating the visual and the auditory. In the example you provided you said something about the invisibility, and of bringing something back into a material mode where you can see it while you're listening. And that tension is precisely what I'm interested in. It's not necessarily a removal of one at the expense of another, but rather a very complicated negotiation of how two interrelate, sync, don't sync, conflict, are antagonistic. I liked a lot of the words that you were using to describe this mode of listening but want to take that and apply it to other things.

Claudia Molitor: It's more than listening and seeing really. There are other things, like the atmosphere in a room, whether it's hot, whether it's cold, whether your shoes are pinching or not, whether you're standing and your back hurts. It might sound frivolous but all of that has an impact on listening, so you can't take the listening and separate it from anything else that we're experiencing. The anthropologist Tim Ingold says we are not in a world full of sounds and visual impacts and touch sensations but the world is full of stuff and we just experience it through our skin, with the ear, with the eye. So it's all incredibly integrated, and that goes back then to experiences of the concert hall, because that will already elicit certain emotions. Going through the door at the Royal Opera House will instantly give you some emotional sensation with which you will then approach the music. But if I go through the hall of the Tate Modern and the same opera is being performed in the Turbine Hall (if it could be sonically identical, which it can't) it would still be a completely different listening experience because I'm already emotionally in a different space.

Allen: As a footnote one should think about the form of our presence here, which bespeaks a certain anti-retinal prejudice [laughter]. You will remember that the last e-mail we got was 'There will be no images only sound', and I had to negotiate the presence of all of this [pointing to the monitor screen].

Nye: I'm afraid that this is probably a legacy of classical music. Actually, it's a legacy of a tradition of music that started to separate instrumental music from theatre.

Allen: But there is opera.

Nye: There is opera.

Cathy Lane: It's also the legacy of being a small sound department in a large art college [long laughter].

Nye: I would get annoyed with students who want to make videos, not because I don't want them to make videos really, but because I think 'learn to listen first', you're sound students. Why does the first thing have to be using Jitter rather than working with sound? But of course one of the interesting things about the emergence of sound art within the visual art community is the reintegration of thinking about sound in terms of its multimodal reality, rather than as an isolated thing that we just do with our ears.

Claudia: But do you think that happens in the classical-music tradition?

Volkmar: That's a very young thing, this isolated, pure sound and music. Mahler's eighth symphony – that's five-hundred resonating vibrating bodies on stage. If you're up there and singing this is a rather bodily affair [laughter] and it always has been. That's why I believe that opera's way of convening together, being beautiful together, is a very strong concept. There is no amplification, it's just bodies. There are no speakers involved, just singers and everybody's moving. That's a sweaty group!

Nye: I'm thinking really of the sort of Schaefferian concepts—

Volkmar: But that's very young.

Nye: Yes, it is very, very recent, but it kind of dominated the early emergence of sound art.

Volkmar: And on the other hand, the symbolic world is in the score only? Like, NO!

[Pause]

Nye: Yes.

Volkmar: No.

[Pause]

David Toop: The thing that unites, for me, what Salomé and Allen have said is that there is another history of listening, which is only just now being written. The *suikinkutsu* fits within that and some of the ideas that Salomé is talking about fit within that. For example, I was just writing a blog in which I discuss Max Wall in his 'Professor Wallofski' incarnation, in which he attempts to approach the piano. I think that that is a great instance of something that conservatoire students should be forced to watch [laughter], because it's about the body in relation to the musical instrument through this codified world of comedy, which, in a sense, is not so very different to the codified world of Zen aesthetics that you're talking about Allen. At the moment we have a history of listening which is founded in factionalism, so it has all of these extra-musical factors that we have heard about today. There is another history of listening which is maybe less factionalised and has the chance to, maybe, unite all of our separateness more effectively, and that takes us beyond these arbitrary distinctions between listening and seeing, because of course we can't separate them. In the end we can't separate out the visual, the body doesn't work like that. In the fullness of time I'm confident that this new history of listening, which can include musical comedians and *suikinkutsu*s, will give us a very different perspective on the environment in which we are all working. Whether we live to enjoy the benefits of that is another matter.

Responses

Abstracts

Nye Parry

Much of the discussion at the Sound Art and Music colloquium focused on the materiality of sound and the act of listening 'in the moment' as an embodied interaction with the sonic. As I observed, this seems strongly at odds with the discourses of classical musicology, and can cause friction within musical institutions dedicated in part to the preservation of a musical culture rooted in the symbolic representation of music as score. In this response I will look deeper at this distinction to tease out a more complex relationship in which the symbolic representation of sound has given rise to a split between conceptions of a transcendental work and its material manifestation in sound. Finally I will discuss how a more sound-led view of the work, tied to the creative use of recording technology, has impacted on discourses of music and sound arts.

David Toop

'I am not interested in dogmatic theories of sound or sound art, nor am I interested in static, one-dimensional histories that are isolated from all other work with sound, or music, or art, or politics, or ways of living. What does interest me: the subtle web of connections and actions through which listening practice and the emanations of sound are articulated, the often arcane trajectory which links the disturbances of sound within the worlds of creatures both living and not.'

David Toop agreed to meet Salomé Voegelin at the café of the Victoria and Albert Museum in London on Wednesday 25th February 2015, to answer three questions on the themes that had come out most strongly from the first session of the colloquium discussions. The interview, which lasted just under one hour and is represented in full here, gives a wonderful account of how the key terms of mythology, traditions and factionalism were important in the early '70s, arguably the beginning of the explorations between sound art and music, for David personally, as well as in more general terms for his peers and the development of sound and art at large.

First Response – Nye Parry

Notation and the Work-Concept in Conceptions of Music and Sound Art

Introduction

In the colloquium that gave rise to this book, I made a comment to the effect that musical institutions such as the conservatoire exist in part to justify a view of music that is based primarily on its symbolic representation in the form of a score. I suggested that the reluctance of these institutions to embrace some of the practices we associate with the emerging field of sound arts could be interpreted as a resistance to the more direct engagement with sound as material which has been brought about by recording, and which, in the context of the colloquium, had been a major theme of the discussion up to this point.

In developing this idea I find that the context for my remarks is highly significant in forming the thought and setting limits on its interpretation, and feel the need first to examine the discussion that led up to my comments. As my contribution dealt in part with the biases of musical institutions, I will then briefly consider the role of institutions in the creation and maintenance of particular interest groups, and how artists use the categories of music and sound art to establish communities and identify with or question certain cultural assumptions.

This I hope will clear the way for me to return to the central question of notation without fear of producing a simplistic dualism of music versus sound art, and explore how the symbolic representation of sound on paper still shapes contemporary ideas on the sonic arts. In particular I will consider how notation has contributed to the establishment of the work-concept in music and how this has impacted on musicology as well as discourses of performance and sound art.

I will suggest that while the materiality of sound informs

musical performance pedagogy and journalistic music criticism, it has to a large degree been sidelined in academic musicology which has favoured an idealised view of the musical work whose meanings are perhaps only partially revealed in performance. I will discuss how a revised conception of sonic materiality, brought about by the increased use of recording technologies, has impacted on musical and sound arts discourses.

Provocations

The opening provocations at the colloquium of Sound Art and Music presented two quite contrasting perspectives on the question of codification.

In the first Allen S. Weiss described how the Japanese *suikinkutsu* (water zither cave) has been re-contextualised, from its origins in the 17th-century tea ceremony where its place in a system of beliefs, philosophies, and rituals contributed to a rich network of signification, to the 21st century in which it has been transformed into the 'mere curiosity of an unusual musical instrument'.

Salomé Voegelin on the other hand structured her presentation around the desire for a mode of listening that would engage directly with the 'materiality' of sound, in the hope that such a listening would allow us to reconsider the breadth of sonic-arts practice, encompassing both (classical) music and contemporary sound art. To this end she was careful to distance herself from both the 'visual / conceptual' theorisation of much sound art criticism and classical musicology with its emphasis on the score, associating the latter with the institutions of music, the conservatoire and the concert hall, which have in her view sidelined much of what has been going on in the sonic arts in the last sixty years.

This brief summary cannot do justice to the complexity of either argument; however it is striking that in Weiss' presentation, the abstracted mode of listening to the *suikinkutsu* in the

21st century was presented as an impoverishment of its meaning, while Voegelin's argument could be interpreted as espousing just such an approach as a way of directly engaging with sonic artworks and bypassing the accumulated baggage of existing theorisations.

It would, however, be simplistic to suggest that such a listening should be equated with some kind of pure phenomenological reduction or unmediated sensation. Both speakers located origins for their re-conceptualisations of the sonic artwork in the experimental music traditions of Edgard Varèse, John Cage, Pierre Schaeffer etc. and in new modes of listening opened up by their work, suggesting that the ability to understand sound as art in material and in fundamentally sonic terms is a culturally determined and historically recent possibility. Nonetheless the discussion that followed these opening provocations picked up on the distinction between a codified form of listening to classical music and a form of listening 'in the moment', which Justin Yang identified with improvised music.[1]

In a sense, then, the discussions in the first session of the colloquium were very much about music, and whether classical music in particular demanded a structural mode of listening and a decoding of musical signs that could get in the way of a direct engagement with sound itself. Volkmar Klien suggested that 'to hear music as sound, is not to hear music at all', likening the process to listening to language. Hearing the sounds of language without attending to their meaning, he suggested, is not only undesirable, but, to a speaker of that language, impossible. Voegelin in contrast suggested that the music of Morton Feldman, for example, is more interesting for what you listen to in the moment, which is retained in the body and is somehow separate from the musical text.

These two positions reflect two competing conceptions of music that occur throughout the history of musical thought and which I will trace below. The first is the concept that musical meaning (at least in the Western classical tradition) resides in the composed work as encoded in the score and is revealed through performance, while the second places greater value on the liveness, the variability, and the materiality of music's realisation in time, viewing compositions more as a framework for musical performance.

Both these conceptions of music play a role in musical education and the underlying assumptions of the institutions of music. In the colloquium I stressed the importance of the former, picking up on Voegelin's criticism of a musical discourse dominated by the score, and its dominance in the 'conservatoire tradition'. I suggested that the institutions of classical music are to an extent dedicated to the preservation of a tradition in which sound is represented symbolically, and that this may cause conflict with newer practices that deal directly with the material of sound, through recording or simply through engaged listening practices. While I do feel that this situation is changing, it is not that long ago that music departments and composition competitions insisted that all submissions of electroacoustic music should be accompanied by a score. (The sound artist Peter Vogel recalls creating his first Reaction Score or Reaktionspartitur to describe the interactions of his sound sculptures in response to the requirements of the Donaueschinger Musiktage (Martin and Gleeson 2011), a practice that ironically became a prominent feature of his practice). More controversially, I find it noteworthy that many of the techniques of the studio composer often seem to gain musicological legitimacy only when transferred back into the instrumental domain via traditional notation, by schools of composition such as spectralism (ring modulator harmonies and additive synthesis) and minimalism (tape loops and phasing). The score still carries enormous cultural weight and clearly the symbolic representation of sound has had a profound effect on how the West has viewed the art of music, and this is indeed reflected in the way theory has been taught in our educational establishments.

However, another interpretation of the role of the conservatoire in particular is also possible. As an institution primarily devoted to the education of performers, it could be argued that a primary purpose of a conservatoire training is to mediate between the score and the materiality of performance. It is to give performers the ability to translate the symbolic score into an acoustic fact, restoring all the features of sound that are lost in transcription: detailed articulation, dynamics and sound production, the evolution of the sound through a single note, the deviations of timing from the strict grid of notational practice.

These potentially conflicting positions live side by side in musical education, theory and practice, and I shall explore them in more detail below. Together they structure our ideas of musical meaning, and the legacies of both inform the development of contemporary sound art. The advent of recording in particular has opened up possibilities both of exploring acoustic materiality in all its detail but also of treating the material of sound as a repeatable text in which sonic symbols stand in relation both to each other and to the wider contexts of culture and experience.

I have taken some pains to locate my comments within the discussion as they occurred at the colloquium, as it would be easy to leave the false impression that clear-cut distinctions between music and sound art could be made on the basis of the mediation of the former through the score, or through some fundamental reappraisal of listening in the development of the latter. In reality, notions of both codification and materiality are woven as a thread throughout the history of Western music and continue to inform the discourses of contemporary sonic arts. Questions of 'in the moment' listening, musical codification, and the role of notation do not really require any concept of a separate category of sound art, so it is worth digressing to consider why these questions come up in this context. For this reason I would like to look at these categories critically before proceeding to examine the effect musical notation has had on listening and its ambiguous role within the institution of the conservatoire.

Institutions and discourses of music and sound art

The Sound Art and Music colloquium was convened to discuss the relationship between music and sound art, with the stated aim to explore both 'reasons to keep them separate', and 'possibilities to build a continuum of theorisation and respond to fissures in mimetic practice' (original email invitation from Salomé Voegelin and Thomas Gardner). The difficulty of dealing with such a brief appears to be one of defining what we actually mean by music and sound art. We are dealing with two very slippery concepts. On the one hand we have music, a term that everybody uses and 'understands' (without necessarily agreeing about what should be included). On the other hand sound art is a relatively new term, which is still the preserve of a relatively small community of artists and academics and which, within that community, often serves precisely to establish a 'difference' between its practices and those of other communities that describe their activities as music. This is important to bear in mind. We are dealing not with the relationship between pure, ontologically distinct categories but with the relationship between discourses. These discourses help to delineate and elucidate different forms of practice. They serve to structure the communities that give rise to them and influence thinking and practice, but they are fluid, complex, and interrelated.

With music and sound art we are looking at overlapping communities. Many sound artists have some form of musical training or a background in musical performance, be it in bands or in the classical field as composers or performers. While some are adamant that they are not 'musicians' many are quite flexible in their own descriptions of their work, pragmatically aligning themselves with whichever community is paying the bills, or (less cynically) choosing to classify different activities as sound art or music according to context or according to which discourse fits them best. The description 'sound artist / composer' appears on many websites.

Nonetheless there seems to be a perceived need for a category of sound art, outside the prevailing discourses of 'music'. A community has emerged that no longer feels at home within the institutions of classical music; one that wishes to broaden its conception of the artistic use of sound in ways to which the established discourses of music seem resistant. It is interesting to consider that where much of the academic literature of classical musicology seeks to define music, to understand what music is (frequently keeping within stated or unstated boundaries of cultural and historical assumptions, or in some of the more interesting recent contributions challenging and examining these assumptions themselves), the literature on sound art and/or sonic art frequently has something of the character of a manifesto, asking what such an art might be or might become. Looking along my bookshelves I see subtitles such as *Toward a Non-Cochlear Sonic Art* (Kim-Cohen 2009), *Towards a Philosophy of Sound Art* (Voegelin 2010), *Beyond Music, Between Categories* (Licht 2007). Ours is a community searching for an identity, drawing on existing categories, frequently opposing them, occasionally envying them, but for the most part, thankfully, celebrating the diversity of influences and contexts open to us and enjoying the multitude of ways sound may be used in artistic expression.

For many, then, the term sound art represents a liberation from the strictures of received practices and entrenched values. The discourses of sound art are perceived as more flexible, the institutions less well defined. While composers such as John Cage tried to extend the scope of music, the institutions are perceived as lagging behind, at best paying lip service to new developments while focusing on the preservation of an existing canon. In many ways it is understandable. The canon contains much that is worth preserving and faces marginalisation amid accusations of elitism. However, all too frequently this leads to a destructive conservatism that excludes all other possibilities and ultimately gives foundation to the very same accusations. Even within the musical 'avant-garde' there is often a belief that only one tradition really counts. We frequently hear complaints that 'no one listens to new music', despite the fact that most teenagers consume little else – it's just not the 'right' new music!

Against this backdrop much of what sound artists want to do seems better described by a new discourse, drawing on interdisciplinarity, materiality, and conceptualism. The discourses of sound art seek to actively differentiate a community of artists and theorists from the traditions that gave rise to its practice – not just those of classical music, but also from the traditions of fine art, poetry, theatre, and architecture – and to find common ground between a range of practices that foreground the artistic use of sound. At some point it would be worth unpicking the relationship between the various communities that have come together under the banner of sound arts, in particular the distinct histories of the separate terms sound art and sonic art. Suffice to say that tensions exist and opinions divide in regards to this emerging grouping.

A review in the *New York Times* is worth quoting here:

> The mainstream's embrace of sound art may mask something peculiar: that even as the field reaches new heights, it's also in crisis. Art-trained figures like Ms. Philipsz and Ms. Cardiff, who build work around the sounds that we care most about — and who resist the whole idea of a coherent genre called "sound art" — are up against a sonic old guard, sometimes including younger figures, that one artist has referred to as the "honk-tweet" school. Aligned with experimental music rather

> than visual art, the honk-tweeters are interested in strange beeps and buzzings for their own sakes. They craft what the sound artist, theorist and blogger Seth Kim-Cohen refers to as purely cochlear, rather than fully mindful, sound art. (Gopnik 2013)

This tension is symptomatic of group formation and echoes the emergence of experimental music itself, described in Benjamin Piekut's *Experimentalism Otherwise*:

> If experimentalism is a grouping, then conflicts are the traces of its formation. As in any case of group formation, this one involves spokespersons who make the group talk, actors who mobilise resources to make boundaries more durable, professionals who authorise the group, and those who map anti-groups. (Piekut 2011, 11)

In the case of sound art, then, we can observe certain 'boundary wars' in which sometimes conflicting views, theorisations and historical precedents are brought to bear by spokespersons keen to define the field in their own image. Importantly for the arguments that follow we can also observe how potentially conflicting conceptions can coexist within a single community, who may use them to highlight different practices or approaches or different interpretations of, and perspectives on, the work under examination.

Within the context of the Sound Art and Music colloquium, for example, two potentially conflicted characterisations of sound art were referenced at different times. The first is the position under discussion, that sound art favours a particular attitude of listening, a direct engagement with the material of sound, an idea closely linked with the Schaefferian 'primacy of the ear' (Schaeffer 1973, 29–30) and often articulated in opposition to the dominance of the visual in contemporary culture. The second position (represented at the colloquium for example by Aura Satz's comments in which she discusses listening as a 'mode of paying attention that is not necessarily tied to the auditory') is the idea of a multi-modal and embodied sound art drawing together the senses and re-integrating listening with a holistic sensorium, one that sees sound art as reversing the tendency of classical music to separate sound from the environment and the body by presenting it as a disembodied, transcendent and purely aural experience.

The work-concept, notation and performance

What these two ideas have in common is that they represent alternatives to a conception of music that became prevalent over the course of the 19th and 20th centuries, and which sees the musical work as somehow divorced from its sounding realisation. A number of factors contributed to this development. Firstly the secularisation of music and the rise of instrumental music as an art form of equal importance to vocal music was crucial to the separation of the aural from the visual, the theatrical and the literary. While opera remained an important force that even, it has been argued (e.g. Small 1998, 147–8), provided narrative archetypes that structured symphonic music, it is noteworthy that opera composers throughout the 19th and 20th centuries spoke of re-uniting music with the other art forms from which it was perceived to have been separated.

Secondly, the possibilities opened up by musical notation, to compose large-scale structures, which could be viewed and overviewed outside of their realisation in performance, divorced from their temporal manifestation as heard music, but understood as a set of symbolic relationships, played into a platonic conception of the musical work as existing ultimately beyond sound itself, which was increasingly prevalent. Nicholas Cook quotes Robin George Collingwood's *The Principles of Art* (1938):

> A piece of music is not something audible, but something which may exist solely in the musician's head (including, of course, the audience as well as the composer under that name), for his imagination is always supplementing correcting and expurgating what he actually hears. The music which he actually enjoys as a work of art is thus never sensuously or 'actually' heard at all. It is something imagined. (Cook 1992, 36)

This platonic view, in which musical performance is a mere token of a musical type that exists either only in the mind or, in its most extreme form, even in some transcendental realm of ideas, where the composer is a mere vessel through which the music passes (e.g. Stravinsky on the *Rite of Spring* in Stravinsky and Craft 1981, 147–8), has been highly influential in shaping the relationship between composers and performers. It is a view of the musical work in which music's 'meaning' resides entirely in the relationships between musical values inscribed in the score. The performer is reduced to a conduit for the composer's intentions and the performance a mere representation of the work of art not the art itself. Indeed, as Collingwood implies in the above quote, the performed work is inevitably a poor copy of the platonic ideal work.

The rise of this musical 'work-concept' as it has been labelled by Lydia Goehr (1992) is a relatively recent phenomenon. Both Goehr herself and Carl Dahlhaus (1982) suggest a date of around 1800 for its full emergence, although its origins can be traced back to Gregorian Chant and the beginnings of notation itself:

> Music is [...] conceived platonically, as an abstract and enduring entity that is reflected in notation, with the notation itself being reflected in singing (since mistakes in singing can be corrected by reference to notation.) (Cook 2014, 11)

This is not to say that the work equates directly to the score. It exists beyond any physical manifestation. However it does appear to be fully defined by the score, so that in the view of Theodor Adorno, 'the entire need for performance disappears if one can read music' (quoted in Cook 2014, 8). This extreme position is of course far from universal but it does reflect the widely held view that the sounds of a piece of music only partially represent the work – that the meaning of the music is fully represented by the notation and, ultimately, that those aspects of the performed work not captured by notation do not contribute to its meaning. Indeed they could even distract from the meanings of the work. This idea is expressed by Collingwood's suggestion that: 'Any concentration on the pleasantness of the noises themselves concentrates the mind on hearing, and makes it hard to listen' (quoted in Cook 1992, 36). This has strong implications for the act of listening. The listener is required to hear past the 'imperfections' of performance, to perceive a work that lies beyond the acoustic reality of performed music. The performer's role is reduced to an attempt to represent the relationships defined in the score as accurately as possible.

An alternative conception: the materiality of performance

A more generous take on performance is represented by the comments of Michael Oliver, who suggests that:

> It can be said that a listener who knows Beethoven's 'Hammerklavier Sonata' very well, from repeated listening to a single fine recording, may in fact know it less well than a concert goer who has heard only two performances of it, but strongly contrasting ones. (Oliver 1999, 253)

This more performance-oriented view seems to be more prevalent among music lovers and critics than in the musicological literature, and it is notable that the above quote is from a popular book by a music critic rather than from an academic paper. Here each individual interpretation sheds new light on the (potential) meanings implied by the score. The performer's role is to illuminate the work and reveal its meanings through performance and the concretisation of the work in sound.

Furthermore, the extent to which the listener experience reflects the formal concerns of the work-concept is itself questionable. Cook's research suggests that the reordering of sections or tampering with the tonal development of a symphonic work has little negative impact on the listening experience even among trained musicians (Cook 1992, 43–70). In fact for most people, the listening experience suggests a much more concrete notion of musical meaning than the work-concept would suggest. Anyone who has ever heard a MIDI realisation of a classical work will know that musical meaning cannot reside only in those aspects of the music that are notated and that the nuances of performance are essential to an appreciation or 'understanding' of music. From the listener's perspective a concert is as likely to be attractive by dint of the performer as it is for the repertoire that is being performed, and a musician may be lauded either for the way they 'understand' a particular score (Barenboim's Beethoven) or alternatively for the way they reinterpret and test our assumptions (Gould's Bach). If the relationships inscribed in the score were the sole carriers of musical meaning, no performer would ever dare to cut a repetition of an exposition or tamper with the tempo markings of a symphonic movement, but these are (or were) common practices in the performance tradition of classical music. This would indicate that within classical music as a practice, a conception of music as performance coexists with the musical work-concept.

The actual experience of music goes beyond an appreciation of 'the work' as defined in notation, and includes all the material considerations of articulation and sound production that are traditionally the domain of the performer. The reality of a conservatoire education in particular is one of understanding not only the relationships between musical symbols, of finding the sonic potential of the score and how it can be translated into actual physical experience, but also an understanding of the instrument and the body, the relationship of phrasing to breath, sound production to muscular tension and relaxation, etc. The role of the interpreter could then be seen as one of bringing to the music all the features of sonic reality that cannot be put on paper. The interpreter concretises the musical abstraction (in Schaefferian terms) dealing directly with the materiality of musical sound.

The work-concept from notation to recording

Despite the obvious importance of performance in the history of classical music, the power of the work-concept has been such that composers have increasingly wanted to bring aspects of performance under their control, to make the material realisation of the score an immutable part of the scored work. John Butt remarks that:

> The traditional periodization of music history tends to support this view of the fully formed work solidifying in the nineteenth century, and of the composer taking ever more control over the notation of performance directives in music. The medieval period was the time when first pitch and later rhythm were notated; in the Renaissance complex tempo relationships were established; in the Baroque, details of expression, tempo, dynamics, ornamentation and articulation were added to the notation; in the classical period diminuendos and crescendos came to be notated and all expressive directions were notated in greater detail and in greater precision; and, with Beethoven, tempo itself could be established with the aid of metronome marks. (Butt 2002, 98)

This desire to bring all aspects of music under the control of the composer continued into the 20th century, most noticeably with the desire of the serialists to create a music in which 'work and material have the same structure' (Stuckenschmidt 1969, 183). This notion takes the platonic work-concept to its ultimate conclusion, a perfectly unified form where every aspect of sound is specified. Karlheinz Stockhausen describes this goal:

> In 1954-55 I wrote several articles in which I suggested the development of all parameters, so that they all would come to have an equal level of importance. This means that we need scales for dynamics, which would have at least 80-90 [sic] precisely measured degrees of dynamics. (Cott and Stockhausen 1973, 91)

That his ambition was thwarted is attributed to the practicalities of notation rather than the importance of performance in the creation of music:

> You can't do everything at once because we no longer have a unified notation. For every sound characteristic we use a different symbol. I tried to find a unified notation so that with one sign I could indicate a sound which has a certain pitch, a certain duration, a certain timbre, a certain loudness, and a certain position in space. But imagine what a complex notation you would need. (Ibid 92)

The date of these musings is telling. They coincide precisely with his earliest experiences at the studios of WDR, where he worked to create just such a unified music, one that did not require the mediation of a performer. Whether the possibilities of electronic music guided his ambitions in this direction, or whether he saw the studio as a tool to realise the perfection of form he sought through his conception of serial technique (most likely both), it is clear that the emergence of tape music, at least in the conception of the serialists, fits perfectly into the composer-led narrative of the romantic work-concept. And indeed Butt's summary of the ever-increasing specificity of notation interestingly continues beyond the list above, putting tape music at the pinnacle of the deterministic trend:

> The same 'story' can be continued to encompass the specification of many other musical and extra-musical factors in performance by Wagner, to Stravinsky's [sic] belief that the performer need do nothing more than read the notated instructions, to the serialization of dynamic and attack by Messiaen, Babbitt and Boulez, and, finally, to tape music and its successors, in which both performer and notation are subsumed by the medium of data storage. (Butt 2002, 98)

The essence of this idea is that the musical meaning resides in a text created by a single individual who should control as many parameters of the sound as possible. Locating meaning in the text requires that the musical experience be repeatable. In notated music this was only possible for relatively few parameters, which were therefore considered the principal carriers of musical meaning. This links them directly to the notion of the transcendent work, for as Cook suggests:

> To hear a symphony as a symphony, to hear a fugue as a fugue – in short, to hear any music as form – is then to hear it as repeatable and hence independent of its realization in sound on any particular occasion. (Cook 1992, 36)

The material reality of sound is accepted as a part of the musical experience but it needs to be tamed and integrated into a work to become truly meaningful. Recording allows sound itself to become repeatable and controlled as part of the process of composition: timbre, dynamics, articulation all become accessible to formal construction and analysis. In this view recording takes the representation of sound in notation to its ultimate conclusion. On tape, every aspect of sound is captured and can be manipulated outside of the temporal flow of live performance.

For the musicologist this has opened up the possibility to closely examine performances as texts. Individual performances can be studied and compared in great detail, bringing performance and interpretation into the purview of musical analysis.

For the composer it has opened up the possibility of manipulating and constructing timbre, dynamics and articulation in greater detail than ever before. We can see the implications of this for the work-concept most clearly in the early works of the Cologne School. Here the medium of tape music fully embraces the prescriptive role of notation. Sound is constructed from scratch and every parameter is controlled. The limitations of this approach are obvious and by the late '50s a more performative studio practice has already overtaken this constructive idealism (see Decroupet, Ungeheuer, and Kohl 1998). (It is also striking that in Stockhausen's music, at least, this experience of absolute control leads very quickly to the adoption of open forms and the reimagining of the role of the performer that is at the heart of works such as *Klavierstück 11* and, later, *Plus Minus* and *Aus den Sieben Tagen*.) However the idea that tape (and presently, the computer) could allow the composer to construct a sonic ideal, rather than investigate a sonic reality, is rooted firmly in the platonic work-concept. The early works of the Cologne School strive to represent a quasi-mathematical perfection, requiring the listener to hear past the imperfections of the tape medium of the day.

At first sight the works of Schaeffer and the Paris School present an alternative view, emphasising direct perception of found sound materials through reduced listening. However reduced listening as an investigation of the characteristics of sound serves in Schaeffer's thought as a first step in the construction of a musical language:

> In musical research also, the concrete *characteristics* of sound are used to try and discover the "pertinent traits" which emerge as abstract musical material, "values", once objects are placed in a structure in accordance with the rule of *permanence of (concrete) characteristics / variation of (abstract) values*. (Chion 2009, 38)[2]

Schaeffer proposes a dualism of values and characteristics to distinguish those aspects of the sound object that contribute to the musical sign system (traditionally pitch and duration) from those that don't. His aim is to identify characteristics of sound that can function as values in such a system.

> Values are the *relevant features,* which emerge from several sound objects placed in a structure and form the elements of the *abstract* musical discourse properly speaking; the other aspects of the object which are not relevant in the musical structure but which form its concrete substance, its matter, are grouped together under the name of *characteristic*. (Ibid 74–5)

For such values to exist they must function within a structure. This allows Schaeffer to distinguish between musicality, the '*abstract* aspect of the musical work' (71), and sonority, the '*concrete* part which can vary with each performance, each embodiment of the work' (Ibid 71). So, as with Stockhausen, it is the repeatability of recording that allows the composer to go beyond the previous limits of notation, to admit other characteristics of sound than pitch and duration to the realm of the musical, and to bring them under the control of the composer. Thus it would be wrong to think of Schaefferian reduced listening as an end in itself, as Kim-Cohen appears to do when he likens Schaeffer's 'overt Husserlianism' (2009, 94) to McLuhan's notion of acoustic space as immersive, non-linear, and sensuous (Ibid 92). For Schaeffer the purely sonorous still resides outside the musical system. His values represent signs in a semiotic system that generates musical meaning, which is essentially abstract.[3]

That said, Schaeffer's writings do emphasise the materiality of sound, making a distinction between the arbitrary signs of language and the values of the semiotics of music. Where 'the value of an element in the linguistic system is purely due to its place in the system, and is not due to any intrinsic property' (Chion 2009, 85). However, '*musical value*, even if it is functional and differential, nevertheless *relies on intrinsic properties of the sound object*' (Ibid).

It is this insight that re-unites a semiotic reading of musical meaning with the concrete reality of sound. It follows that music can only exist in its sounded form, be it in the playback of a recording or in live performance of a scored composition. Consequently, Schaeffer makes a point of differentiating the musical sign, consisting of values identified in the sound object, from its representation in '*a notation which misleads us, by making us think that it is a sign which exists before its realization*' (Ibid 88).[4] This is a profound rejection of the platonic role of notation as a description of an ideal musical work divorced from its sonic manifestation.

Conclusion

The distinction, presented at the beginning of this response, between a symbolic listening, focusing on the relationships of sounds in a structure, and an 'in the moment', experiential mode of direct engagement with sound as a material, is perhaps not as clear-cut as it might seem. Music unfolds in time and thus engages our memories and our ability to predict future events. If the music of Feldman seems to hold us in the present moment, is this not a function of how the sounds are organised in time? Do improvisers not keep their listeners attention through a careful, albeit spontaneous, manipulation of expectations? While in the normal course of events music is encountered as sound, the prevalence of the transcendent work-concept suggests that its meanings lie beyond the materiality of the object of perception, the musical performance. This has had consequences for composers, performers and audiences alike. For composers it has led to the desire to close down any possibilities for 'mis-reading' of the musical text, any chance that the performer may fail to reproduce the transcendental work. For performers it has led to an over-stated emphasis on authenticity and truth-to-the-work, and for audiences it has had the unfortunate effect of leading to a fear of hearing a work the 'wrong' way, a sense that you don't 'understand' a piece of music if you can't identify its modulations' structural units.

Furthermore the confusion, identified by Schaeffer, between the written symbols of notation and musical signs consisting of actual sounds in relation to one another in a piece of experienced music, has led many musicologists to sideline performance and the network of meanings brought into play at the moment of a work's realisation.

For the performers themselves, sound has always been the material of their art. Where composers and musicologists may have been seduced by the score and the manipulation of symbols on the page, performers have created sound in time bringing the musical work into being at each performance. As Carolyn Abbate argues:

> Musical sounds are made by labor. And it is in the irreversible experience of playing, singing, or listening that any meanings summoned by music come into being. Retreating to the work displaces that experience. (Abbate 2004, 505)

Beyond academia it is not so much that the (classical) musical world ignores performance, but that it inherits the assumption that the functions of composer and performer are separate and distinct, and that performance, while it may celebrate the materiality of sound and the body in the beauty of tone and virtuosity of execution, ultimately serves as a temporary embodiment of transcendent platonic works, somehow (mystically) brought into being by composers.

The availability of recorded sound has made what was ephemeral repeatable, and indeed malleable, collapsing the roles of composer and performer. But more than this, it has established a new kind of relationship between the composer and the sonic reality of the performed (or reproduced) work. Stockhausen's dream of the composer controlling all the parameters of sound, bringing them into the realm of the score, 'realised' in the electronic-music studio, is challenged by the very materiality of sounds, by their resistance to certain manipulations and transformations and their ability to suggest directions and relationships during the work process. Composition with recorded sound becomes a dialogue with the material, in which the composer responds as well as controls. In reality of course this has always been a part of composition (and performance), but recorded sound makes this aspect of musical creation explicit and leads many composers to accept a more responsive relationship with their materials. This re-definition of the role of the composer in relation to the material of sound forces us to rethink the musical work-concept. Far from being a transcendent ideal the musical work can only exist as sound at the moment of its realisation, the moment of perception. It is, in Schaeffer's terms, concrete!

It is perhaps the reluctance of musical institutions to make this leap that has led many composers to seek to re-define themselves as sound artists or sonic artists. Trevor Wishart for example complains of 'the rejection by some musicians and musicologists of my work on the grounds that "it is not music"' (Wishart 1996, 4).

For composers such as Wishart, a discourse drawing in part on traditions of fine art may seem more appropriate to the material concerns of their work. For them the platonic work-concept has been replaced by an active engagement with sound as a material; an engagement in which the material has a direct bearing on the resultant form. This revised work concept proposes no transcendent ideal revealed through performance or interpretation. Instead the object itself embodies the work. This relationship with material and the object aligns well with certain conceptions of the object in fine art, particularly in traditional notions of sculpture.

However, the fine-art community has itself struggled with an evolving work-concept. The history of the work-concept in fine art and its influence on the sound arts community will have to wait for another time. It suffices to say that where musicology is beginning – in the work of such writers as Abbate, Butt, and Cook – to re-engage with the materiality of performance, recent conceptions of fine art, such as Bourriaud's relational aesthetics (Bourriaud 1998), have moved ever further away from a material conception. It is noteworthy also that the admission of performance (and to a lesser extent, sound art) into the pantheon of fine-art genres has been a key factor in these developments. This sheds some light on the debates within the sound art community discussed earlier. Where for many composers a direct engagement with sound has produced a heightened awareness of its materiality, for some artists with roots in contemporary fine art, the idea that art can be made from such an ephemeral material as sound confirms a post-retinal (dare I say transcendent?) conception of the artwork in the realm of ideas.

The possibilities opened up by recording technologies in the last century have had a profound effect on our engagement with the material of sound. For scholars performances have become repeatable and analysable texts, raising questions about the contribution of performance to musical-meaning formation; while for composers the ability to work with sounds without the mediation of a written language has led to a fundamental questioning of the nature of musical and sonic creation and to the emergence of new communities around the creative possibilities this has opened up.

Bibliography

Abbate, Carolyn. 2004. 'Music—Drastic or Gnostic?' *Critical Inquiry* 30 (3): 505–36. doi:10.1086/421160.

Bourriand, Nicholas. 1998. *Relational Aesthetics*. Dijon: Les Presses Du Reel.

Butt, John. 2002. *Playing with History: The Historical Approach to Musical Performance*. Cambridge University Press.

Chion, Michel. 2009. 'Guide to Sound Objects: Pierre Schaeffer and Musical Research.' Trans. John Dack and Christine North. Institut National De L'audiovisuel & Éditions Buchet/Chastel. http://www.ears.dmu.ac.uk/IMG/pdf/Chion-guide/.

Cook, Nicholas. 1992. *Music, Imagination, and Culture*. New ed. Oxford; New York: Oxford University Press.

—. 2014. *Beyond the Score: Music as Performance*. New York: Oxford University Press USA.

Cott, Jonathan, and Karlheinz Stockhausen. 1973. *Stockhausen: conversations with the composer*. New York: Simon and Schuster.

Dahlhaus, Carl. 1982. *Esthetics of music*. Cambridge; NY: Cambridge University Press.

Decroupet, Pascal, Elena Ungeheuer, and Jerome Kohl. 1998. 'Through the Sensory Looking-Glass: The Aesthetic and Serial Foundations of Gesang Der Jünglinge.' *Perspectives of New Music* 36 (1): 97. doi:10.2307/833578.

Goehr, Lydia. 1992. *The Imaginary Museum of Musical Works: An Essay in the Philosophy of Music*. Oxford University Press.

Gopnik, Blake. 2013. 'Museums Embrace Works Made of Sound.' *The New York Times,* August 1, sec. Arts / Art & Design. http://www.nytimes.com/2013/08/04/arts/design/museums-embrace-works-made-of-sound.html.

Kim-Cohen, Seth. 2009. *In the Blink of an Ear: Toward a Non-Cochlear Sonic Art.* 1st ed. Continuum Pub Group.

Licht, Alan. 2007. *Sound Art: Beyond Music, Between Categories.* Har/Com edition. New York, N.Y: Rizzoli.

Martin, Jean, and Conall Gleeson. 2011. *Peter Vogel – The Sound of Shadows.* DVD. Wergo.

Nattiez, Jean-Jacques. 1990. *Music and Discourse: Toward a Semiology of Music.* Princeton University Press.

Oliver, Michael. 1999. *Settling the Score: A Journey Through the Music of the Twentieth Century.* London: Faber & Faber.

Piekut, Benjamin. 2011. *Experimentalism Otherwise: The New York Avant-Garde and Its Limits.* Berkeley: University of California Press.

Schaeffer, Pierre. n.d. *La Musique Concrète éd 1973.* Presses Universitaires De France – Puf.

Small, Christopher. 1998. *Musicking: The Meanings of Performing and Listening.* 1st ed. Wesleyan University Press.

Stravinsky, Igor, and Robert Craft. 1981. *Expositions and Developments.* New ed. Berkeley: University of California Press.

Stuckenschmidt, H. H. 1969. *Twentieth Century Music.* New York: WORLD UNIV LIBRARY.

Voegelin, Salomé. 2010. *Listening to Noise and Silence: Towards a Philosophy of Sound Art.* Bloomsbury Publishing.

Wishart, Trevor. 1996. *On Sonic Art.* Amsterdam: Harwood Academic Publishers.

Notes

1 It is worth noting that the discussion focused on what Nattiez (1990, 115) calls intrinsic codification, consisting of relation-

ships within the musical work, while Weiss' provocation suggested a much broader system of cultural codification. While this distinction is highly pertinent to debates within the sound art and music communities it will only be touched on in the present response.

2 All quotes relating to Schaeffer are taken from Chion's *Guide Des Objets Sonores* in the translation by Dack and North available from http://www.ears.dmu.ac.uk/IMG/pdf/Chion-guide/

3 Schaeffer's system of signs does however function purely intrinsically (see footnote 1) – any extra-musical reference is explicitly excluded.

4 This is a direct quote from Schaeffer's *Traité des Objets Musicaux*, p.288.

Second Response – David Toop

Interviewed by Salomé Voegelin at the V&A: seeing Harpo Marx play the piano, destroy it, and play it as a harp

Salomé Voegelin: David, thanks for agreeing to meet me here and answer some questions that arose from the colloquium discussions. I will begin right away with my first question:

One of the topics that came out of Allen S. Weiss' provocation, which discussed the *suikinkutsu* (water zither cave) and the Japanese tea ceremony, was the notion of myth, mythology. The discussion that ensued was about myth and content, myth or content.

Where is myth in your work, or in your perception of sound art and music? Do we need a myth?

David Toop: I used to feel that I needed a personal myth. When I first began thinking about sound and listening as activities that started to float away from music, and this would have been at a very pivotal time for me – 1971/72 – I got very strongly into myth. One of the things I was interested in was the context of sound and listening and how listening had been understood in societies described by anthropology or comparative religion; or how it functioned in extra-human societies.

I used to come here, for example, to the V&A in the early '70s, to the library to read about bioacoustics, and I used to go up the road to the sound archive, where it used to be, to listen to otherwise-unavailable recordings of howler monkeys, seals, and cetaceans. All of this, I now see in retrospect, was the construction of a personal myth. The engine that was driving this research was also driving me out into a cold and lonely place in fact, so I needed something to sustain me. Because there were very few other people who were thinking that way about sound at the time, there was no support mechanism, no recognition, so I needed some kind of myth. There was a circularity in this process. I looked in anthropology, for example, to find situations in which sound was seen to be meaningful, or where listening was a highly integrated part of ordinary life, not a special thing but an important way of perceiving the world. One of the prime ways of creating a myth for myself was by thinking in terms of what Sigmund Freud called 'the oceanic': this kind of going-back into the womb, the mother's womb, this aqueous environment that translated in psychological terms into an environment without boundaries. A lot of music and a lot of bioacoustics sounds seemed to express that for me. So it was a complicated thing – going on with constructing my own myth – because I needed that sustenance of delving into other people's myths in order to find something that felt meaningful. I think the motivation for that connects with what Allen S. Weiss is talking about when he mentions the Japanese *suikinkutsu*.

There was a frustration with music as entertainment. The improvisation scene that Paul Burwell and I got involved in, almost by default, was a small group of people who were saying no to music as entertainment. The purpose of that was not to become a very esoteric sect but to say this entertainment business has disconnected music from notions of democratisation or anything meaningful in people's life: music is just something people listen to as an escape. Whereas we wanted to know how it connects to the practice of daily life, with listening practice, how it might contribute to the creation of a different kind of society in which people, men, women, different races, different beliefs, have a more meaningful relationship? So that was a big ambition for people who were getting involved in a music that basically nobody cared about.

The question was: how is sound meaningful? How can we think differently about the perception of sound in a world that is highly visuocentric? I had been to art school, and already at art school I was thinking about sound, 1967/68. I was sitting at a table opposite Stuart Marshall, and we were talking about sound, experimental music, and free jazz. For the task of the day we were drawing life models, or drawing objects, but our thinking was very much about listening and sound. So all of these things were mixing together. And in 1971 I wrote a letter to the BBC – talking about sound in an ecological sense – as a twenty-one/twenty-two year old saying to the BBC that I felt they had a responsibility to promote this idea. Which I felt they had done in the past, but so many musics were disappearing along with disappearing species and there was a feeling of alienation in daily life, I felt that the BBC had a role to play in a Reithian sense of public service. So this absurdly self-confident, but not confident at all, letter went into the BBC and eventually a fantastic reply came back from a BBC 3 archive producer called Madeau Stewart. She was very aristocratic but totally sympathetic to me and to what I was saying and secretly held these same beliefs. She had worked with Daphne Oram, in the late 1950s, making drama with electronic sounds. I think they were the two pioneers actually, these two women, who were both quite mystical, you know, they believed in Atlantis and some quite strange stuff. They started experimenting with sound. There were a number of people who I think of as mentors at that time, and Madeau was one of them – she was incredibly encouraging to me. She had a strong sense of history, she was the person who rescued the V&A musical-instrument collection. She came across it mouldering away in corridors and cupboards and told them they had to rescue these instruments and put them on display.

She was related to the Mitford sisters, so she used to go to Inch Kenneth – the island in the north of Scotland where the Nazi Mitford – Unity – used to run up a swastika. Madeau was not a Fascist by any means – quite the opposite – but she was just related to these mad sisters. But she used to go out in a boat in

Scotland and play flute to the seals. I mean I discovered this later, but she had been doing this in the 1950s, this incredibly posh, seemingly establishment woman, so she wasn't so establishment after all. Anyway, she said to me: do you want to make a programme? And she let me loose on the BBC sound archive. They used to allow me to take records home and listening to this treasure trove of recordings I developed an understanding of the diversity of music. I made a programme and the mythical drive behind that programme was that everything is connected. I didn't want to speak during the programme; I just wanted the sounds, those examples pulled out of the BBC sound archive of sounds that were interconnected in various ways. There were musics from various places – Africa, Papua New Guinea, Malaysia, Indonesia – that were imitating animal sounds or bird sounds, and there were animals that were imitating humans, Mynah birds that were imitating humans, and shamanistic rituals with people imitating birds. These were intuitive connections between types of musics. I wanted the sounds and their connections to just appear, just to emerge as a transmission, as if from some other planet. But Madeau said, no, you can't do that, you have to speak. So I just said four cryptic sentences, which probably made the programme more confusing than it would have been if I'd said nothing at all. But that was a real beginning for me because everything that followed was about this idea of connectivity, so *Ocean of Sound* was about the connectivity of different kinds of music in the 20th century, without conventional categorisations or hierarchies of different styles and genres of music or sound. I felt that they are all connected and I could also see connections with extra-human sounds.

I find it very hard to say what that all meant. If anybody cares after I die they can figure it all out, but it was definitely the building of a personal myth. I made a piece that was very important to me in 1971. It was just a text piece, and that was a beginning – my version of what is now called sound art. There was no such thing as sound art then. This piece – Bionic Rock – was making a connection between the inaudible sounds of bats and a particular guitar pedal I was using, a very extreme distortion pedal that made these clicking sounds which were very similar to the sounds that bats made once you pitch-shifted them down in frequency so that humans could hear them. I connected that with the science of bionics, the science of systems based on living things, and so I created this new science called 'bi/s/onics' – the science of sound systems based on living things. It was a kind of nonsensical science, the creation of a myth founded in connections that were totally personal.

Also, my partner at that time, Marie Yates, was an artist. At the beginning of the 1970s we used to do these walks on Dartmoor in Devon, and in Cornwall, and for her the walking practice was the work itself. She would construct a sculpture at the point of arriving in the walk, a sculpture from material we would take with us and then put up or take away, or a sculpture from something that was found on site and would be destroyed very quickly by the weather. So these works were very ephemeral.

Salomé: This leads very interestingly to another issue that came up during this colloquium session, which was the notion of traditions. Getting rid of traditions, continuing traditions or subverting traditions. What do you think about traditions?

David: Traditions are very interesting. The way Marie and I were working was in a sense doing away with traditions, because we were making work that couldn't easily be documented and could not last. The way she dealt with that as an artist was to write out what we had done, in a sort of poetic way, editing both of us out of the work and she would photograph what happened. So she would talk about me making sound but not mention me.

She lives in Crete now but we are still in touch, even though we split up in 1975. Recently we talked about collaborating on a book, and it's extremely difficult because the question of authorship comes into it. For a long time this work has been available by her online as her work, and I have written about it as my work too. And there is an uncomfortable power imbalance because I have a bigger reputation than she does now, and I live in London and she lives in Crete. You can see how difficult it is. And she is a woman who is trying to retrieve some kind of reputation as an artist from working in a time when women were rarely valued as artists. We had some very awkward conversations by email. But there was, in our work, this strong connection with traditions. For me there was a very powerful connection with traditions when I spend so much time in the BBC sound archive. And I also started to make flutes. I was playing electric guitar and flute, working with Paul Burwell, and we became interested in all these musical and shamanistic traditions, which somehow undermined the idea of music as entertainment. In shamanistic cultures certain people went through psychosomatic crises, then became very important within their community as outsiders, and as mediators to a world that most people believed in but did not have the time, the inclination, or the personality to actually engage with. That was interesting to us because the music we were working in was quite ecstatic – sometimes it took us to places that were disturbing and extreme in a psychosomatic way and I think we experienced things through the music which were new to us and unsettling, the kind of conditions that you would call trance, and it was a question of dealing with that and trying to place our music somewhere, because it had no real place in this society. We were playing to a couple of people in tiny clubs, places like the Little Theatre Club, to basically our partners and a few enthusiasts, a couple of other musicians. So it was very difficult. Also we were moving into areas where things were really unknown, so that need for grounding was quite intense and we were looking back to these traditions for that grounding. A lot of people were doing the same at that time. For example, we were going back to this idea of the oceanic – a feeling of melting away into the environment; this intense desire to somehow be strongly connected to the environment in an atmosphere where a lot of artwork was more to do with alienation.

I was listening, for example, to sacred flute music from Papua New Guinea which I had heard on BBC Radio 3, a programme by an Australian anthropologist who had recorded the flutes in the Sepik region. On first hearing, it was a music which seemed to have no boundaries. That was what I was looking for and what I am still looking for. I am always looking for ways to go beyond the boundaries. And that is what that music did to me. So I started making flutes in about 1972. There is a fantastic book by Karl Gustav Izikowitz called *Musical Instruments of the South American Indians*. It was very expensive – being completely broke in those days I stole it from a bookshop, I'm ashamed to say. It was full of drawings and so the flutes were based on these drawings, and sometimes they made only one sound. That was interesting – the idea of making just one sound. I was listening to a lot of music from Papua New Guinea and Amazonas, Brazil, in which people were playing big flutes, in which they were just playing overtones, one-note music, coming down to fundamentals. And of course we are talking about an era in which serialism still existed, this fanatically complex mathematical music which was about permutations of pitches so complicated that in a work like Boulez' *Le marteau sans maître*, it sounded great but the structure was... you needed to be a mathematician to understand it. And so one note was incredibly appealing. But again to play one note put you out on this frozen lake, like you were the last polar bear on the frozen ice. So there was an aspect of taking inspiration, but there was also a sense that you could find meaning in traditions that were fantastically remote and disappearing and had very little to do with somebody who had grown up as a lower middle-class boy in the suburbs of London.

Salomé: Another issue that came up centrally in the colloquium discussions, and you yourself mentioned it, was factionalism. You talked about the post-factional and post-factionalism. And I wondered, what do you really mean by that, has it got to do with traditions? I hoped you could tell me what you mean by the post-factional in relation to what we just talked about now, and in terms of the relationship between music and sound art that was discussed on the day?

David: I see one of the important things about music, the making of music, listening to music, is identity. People identify very strongly with music, for a variety of reasons: they can identify with it physically, they can identify with it very strongly emotionally, they can identify with it as a way of saying this is who I am, this is who you can identify me as. My feeling was I did not want any of the available identities, or I thought I didn't. I was not extreme about it. I still wanted to be a man for example, but I didn't want to be a man's man. I didn't want to be transgender, I mean you could go that way. I didn't want to be locked into masculinity, I could see that I couldn't avoid being a white person, but I saw all of these identities as being divisive, exclusive, or subject to oppression. So how could you confuse your identity for yourself and for other people by using sound? Factionalism was very strong at that time in music. It was very class-based. I used to work in areas where people were consciously brought together: jazz musicians and classical players, so-called classical players. For example, I performed in an Eddie Prévost piece called *Spirals* where he brought together twenty or thirty musicians from all these areas, the improvisers and experimental-music players. We did a performance in Birmingham and I remember getting on the coach afterwards, and all the young classical players were reacting with horror to what had happened. It had turned into a free jazz session. It was this very evident class thing, the experimental-music players were all very middle-class, they had all gone through music college, and the jazz players tended to be working-class, very few of them had gone through higher education at all. They had gone straight from boring jobs into trying to make a living as a jazz musician. They all ended up in the same place.

This factionalism was very strong. Is this jazz or is this art, and if it is art what kind of art is it? I was working with people who were fighting against this – could we say these divisions? I was working with Bob Cobbing, for example, who was a sound poet. Was he a poet or was he a musician, was he this, was he that? And he would always say no, I am not this, I am not that. He could be quite aggressive about what he wasn't but then he was very clear about what he was as well. And then I got to know John Latham and with John it went even deeper. It was like our whole worldview was wrong – in a space-based world it is impossible to reconcile mass and matter with time – so let's think about event structure! This was all happening to me in one or two years. Meeting all these people, working with all these people, making all these discoveries – this was all formative. Who I am now is very much based on those couple of years of intense deconditioning, a deconstruction of myself. And all the people I was working with, we were all working in a similar way; we were all working in areas that had no place in the factions of the time, had no name. Of course in a career sense it was very, very hard for all of us. At the end of John's life very few people took him seriously. Some sort of revival has been underway since his death. Bob ended up in penury. This week I am writing an essay about working with Bob for a Bob Cobbing reader, the grandchildren are taking on that task of honouring his work. Marie has become very isolated in Crete trying to claw back some recognition. Paul Burwell drank himself to death. John Stevens died of a heart attack in his forties, desperately broke as far as I know. I've managed to become respectable, in some ways, and make a career out of all of this, which does sometimes cause me a certain amount of guilt. But I feel I still work on this idea of factionalism. I don't see it as anti-factionalism, that creates another faction, which is simply not called factionalism. I see it as constantly pushing at the desire to fix things. And you and I and Daniela have talked about this, that people are constantly trying to make canons and are constantly trying to fix and tidy up activity. It's important to constantly push at the boundaries of that.

So, for example, it's very interesting to work with Rie Nakajima now. Rie and I have become incredibly close and we are extremely supportive of each other and push each other and I have gone further and further into this boundary condition. Mieko Shiomi made this fantastic piece in 1963 – *Boundary Music* – which is always associated with Fluxus but I don't know whether I see it as a Fluxus piece. It has a different character. It is a hard piece – making a sound on the edge of a boundary condition – so sound may not sound or it may sound. We do this piece with improvisation students sometimes at the London College of Communication and they find it very difficult because what does it mean? I ask myself, what does it mean to work on the edge of a boundary condition? That is what I do with Rie. Paul Burwell and I stopped working together in about 1975 – I have this terrible habit of moving on all the time, when I want to stop working with people. It's about this boundary condition, it's about things getting fixed and in a way it's a horrible thing. It creates terribly difficult personal situations. But Paul and I stopped working together because I felt it was not doing anything. We worked together again in the late '70s and by that time all our instruments had moved down onto the floor. This is really interesting to me because I've gone back to working on the floor. There is something about chairs and tables, something about the bourgeois life, about being European, whereas when you work on the floor suddenly you lose the edges of what you are doing and it becomes rather abject. Abject is also a boundary condition and a fashion in art, so that has its dangers as well. But maybe humility is part of it, saying that the instrument we are working with is not terribly important, it's not a Stradivarius. In my case I have a fantastic Fender Telecaster guitar, which is probably very valuable, but it's not about that fetishisation of the object, it's about thinking that these objects have almost no tangibility. I did a performance in the Christian Marclay exhibition [at the White Cube in Bermondsey 28 January–18 April 2015] where I used glass as a circle. I used the glasses in the exhibition to define a territory. There is another myth if you like, transparency and glass. The last exhibition John Latham did at the Lisson Gallery before he died, I did a sound piece for that exhibition with him, and most of his exhibition was glass. Glass, that transparency is symbolic, and Rie did a performance in Christian's exhibition last Saturday and she just put all of these vibration motors on long cables in the middle of the gallery, then took them out into the audience and put them into glasses. I just thought, Rie is always ahead of me and I like that. You work with somebody and they are always ahead of you and they are always saying, yes we can go one step further. And in terms of age, I am sixty-five now, you are supposed to retire! So you have to work harder and harder to find this boundary condition, this kind of factionless position.

So, coming back to your question about traditions: in the 1970s we had to work through this question of traditions, what did it mean? And this became a political question. You couldn't just take somebody else's tradition. Identity politics were very strong at that time, so it became a very delicate issue. Whole communities were fighting for their identities and losing their identity. They did not want somebody else coming along and appropriating it. And now we've come to this point in history and we talk about archives. So, as you know, we go to conferences about the problems of archiving this kind of activity. The work Marie and I did, in 1971 and 1972, going out onto moorland with a cheap mono cassette recorder and a camera and making work designed not to last, becomes a site of anxiety for the archivist. 'Oh my god this work was not properly documented, what can we do about it, we are losing it all? Quick, it's all going.' And age is a dangerous factor in this because people want you to deal with your own archive constantly. You are fighting your own tradition. Who you are becomes increasingly well-established and -defined. I am fortunate in the sense that I do many things. People think: 'He wrote a book about hip-hop, I hate hip-hop. Why did he do that?' Or they think the opposite, 'I love hip-hop, why is he doing all this other weird stuff about the sound of painting?' And so being ill-defined is advantageous in the broader sense, helping you to constantly chip away at factionalism. If we are talking about this entity of sound art, which is an economic entity, an archival entity, a museological entity, and an identity entity, then I say – and this applies to music as well – I say well, when we were growing up we were not listening to the works of the Futurists. We didn't know about Futurist noise, let's be honest. We knew about Futurist painting maybe but we didn't know about Futurist sound. What we were doing was watching, say, a Marx Brothers' film, seeing Harpo Marx play the piano and destroy it completely as he played it, and then pick up the frame and play it as a harp. This made a huge impression on me. Now am I going to say that is not important because it's comedy, not sound art, or am I going to admit that that was a completely new way of thinking about the instrument and sound? This is something that interests me deeply these days – the idea of the instrument that is not an instrument, in other words the 'beyond the object' principle. I remember seeing this comedy of sound as a child because the Marx Brothers' films used to show frequently on TV in those days, and now we can go back to it on YouTube and watch it and I can write about it in my new book, and I can speak to others and they remember it too. And to me it's important to move outside a canon of sound art full of old Fascists and Nazi sympathisers. I don't want that. I want to go back to these Jewish Liberals, who were interested in what was happening in the Soviet Union.

PART TWO:

Commodification, Rhythms, and Experience

Provocations

Abstracts

Volkmar Klien

Music is a faith-based community. It is a portable home, which is why so many people these days carry it around in headphones. Music helps put things into order. It strives to frame the social situation it evolves in and knows no outside position. Music (with all its links to dance, language, rites, and shopping centres) leads listeners into the moment, because it is there that – in blissful unawareness – eternity takes place.

Musical composition that claims high intellectual standards finds itself in a strange place: reflection on music seems to remain impossible inside the musicking community.

It is my conviction that musical composition cannot sensibly limit itself to the production of work composed in the defined formats of established standards. Rather it should be understood and practiced as a truly open-ended process. For this to happen it is necessary that music invites itself onto a bigger playing field, spanning music and the (in)audible, allowing for new situations and potentially creating novel positions for everyone and everything involved: composers as well as listeners.

Cathy Lane

Music and sound art are often thought of as two ends on the continuum of creative exploration afforded by sound. I suggest that a fracture between them occurs when the artefacts of sounding art enter the commodification process and the work is claimed for one of the two, now separated, conceptual and critical frameworks, which know or understand little of each others' discourses. In this short provocation I show how this drive to differentiate between sound art and music limits the possibilities for artistic expression.

First Provocation – Volkmar Klien

Consonances, Community, and Reflexivity: remarks on the relationship of music and the (sound) arts

For my provocation to start this second session of the colloquium I would like to outline my conviction that music is a faith-based community, and articulate the need for artistic practice in music and sound to remain an open-ended process.

I contend that all attempts to normatively define specific art forms have proven to be futile, utterly impossible and – above all – more obstructive than helpful to artists. The artists themselves have no need to define their object of investigation or their methods of production as a pre-requisite of their practice. The lack of definition cannot be seen as art's deficiency when compared to science or other forms of rigorous research; instead it is its central advantage, because it is specifically this lack of stringent method that allows and requires the search for new ways to create, as well as to perceive. This is why I am not worried if a specific or all of my projects are classified as sound art or music.

Still, as an artist coming from the field of musical composition I have always been intrigued by the relationship between music and its contexts: those that represent established musical standards and expectations, and those that reflect its audible consonances outside of what is traditionally understood as the musical domain. This wider interest in contextual positioning of one's own music-making relates not only to the sounding aspects of music, its sonic material, but also to related practices, traditions, rites, and movements of performing and perceiving, as well as to the ways music shapes our lives, and conversely, how our lives, bodies, and pre-conceptions shape our musical practice.

When shifting one's focus away from the scores and mixing consoles to look into this extended context of musical practice, it becomes obvious that even the 'purest' forms of music are not about structural relations of frequencies in time, but are bodily affairs, linked to all and everything. If we consider the score in isolation there is simply no way to investigate, to give just one example, the fundamentally puzzling, even confounding relationship between the symbol printed on paper and the actual, individual, sound-producing act of the performing musician. In the context of musical conventions and expectations, putting down the first note of an orchestral score means implicitly agreeing to uncountable rules, regulations, and concepts on how to structure the specific work in question. By extension these rules and regulations also determine how to understand and maintain the structures and concepts of a concurrent society, while there are very limited ways to react to these social structures within the score. This relationship between aesthetic practice and social reality means that composing in an extended field, beyond the hermeneutics of a musical context, not only opens up the doors of dedicated venues to new sound worlds, but goes beyond the sonic, to lead to questions on perceiving, moving, and communing within the everyday: it introduces the social dimension of what music is and in doing so connects music – from a fundamentally sonic 'perspective' – to all aspects of the audible and, ultimately, the inaudible, that which is not heard in itself, but is linked to the heard by various forms of cultural construct.

Even though my aim is not the neat delineating of music from other forms of art, but rather its opposite – the understanding of music as integrated implicitly into social mores and habits – I still believe that there exists something we could call 'music proper'. This music proper differentiates itself from sound as sound and it is not fully described by the terms 'organised sound' either.

Language, to give one example that illustrates my issue with the term 'organised sound', is organised sound too; it is not music however, and sound as sound is not music because it lacks the aspect of intended human communication.

To be more specific about the term music I contend that music always evolves as a faith-based community. It creates portable homes, often now carried in headphones. Music helps put things into order and strives to frame the social situation in which it evolves. Making as well as listening to music implies participation in a group activity, and knows no outside position. Participation in these groups today does not require physical presence but can – and more often than not does – take mediated forms. Music is a signpost to the moment where – in communion with others – eternity takes place.

Music allows you to frame how you experience the world. It holds the potential to function as horizon, sealing your world from that of others, or from the terror of the void. Taking along your musical community on headphones helps keep things in proper order, allowing the new to take its place among well-established grids. Music, on headphones or not, dominates the listeners' appreciations of their surroundings, it rules the environment the listeners are situated in or walk through. It does so not only by filling its physical environment with sound, which of course any sound does. Rather, it is a constant, unsolicited and hence intrusive invitation to join in.

I contend that in dominating its social environment, music increases group cohesion. In the age of mediated presence this group is – of course – not necessarily the group you are in or physically closest to; headphones allow for a 'remote log-in' to your community of choice. I also suggest that music provides means of ruling the future: this is the role of the drummer, the function of rhythm and the might of the steady pulse. The more often events in the present play out in ways rather similar to the recent past, the more stable the world becomes, confidence increases and predictions about the near future become more feasible. Communal faith in the stability of the world increases and with it the security and freedom perceived. Structuring time in musical ways helps synchronise people into one train of events, creating a shared chronology, which in turn has direct effects on the concerted experience of causality, its close cousin. Establishing one line of chronology makes the world a more consequential place. One thing happens after the other, and if this repeats often and regularly enough one event will cause another, introducing necessity where in the beginning there only was incidental succession of individual events. In this way music is instrumental in raising the perceived level of security. It allows you to safely join in and take part in society, free of all imminent threats.

Music's might to entrain groups and build a communal faith has shaped theory as well as compositional practice of the European post-war avant-garde in rather specific ways. Many of the implicit rules stemming from this discourse still resonate in the composition departments throughout continental Europe. In Austria and Germany, after the catastrophe of the Nazi period, music with its rumoured powers to synchronise listeners into will-less masses was treated with suspicion. Forms of music with a steady beat and the marching of armies were seen and heard in close alignment. Conscientious composers would not be content with luring their audiences into blissful ignorance and thoughtless communality with the help of harmonies and rhythms. Instead composers tried to introduce reflexive breaks into their musical works, to start an informed discourse with their audience rather than simply showering them with sentiment. The new ideal became an analytical, a structural listener, who behaved in a reflective manner toward the musical composition presented; and the musical works presented did not allow simple consumption through indulgence in a synchronous communal existence. In certain ways the musical avant-garde can be interpreted as an attempt to transcend music in and through music.

The compositional approaches of the avant-garde, aimed at keeping group entrainment at bay, might have succeeded for specific works and concert situations. However, it is safe to say that they have not led to a fundamental change of what music is and how music works in most if not all parts of society: music still has a beat, a melody, and a harmony, and these characteristics are still shaped by their cultural contexts. Music is something you grow up into, it is bigger than you and will always shape you more than you will shape it. Deconstructing the musical community means putting a halt to this cultural predetermination: calling into question the faith in the musical moment while defying it at the same time.

My suspicion is that music proper has rather limited means of incorporating reflection and therefore subversion. Whatever one does as a composer attempting to negotiate difference (in styles, sounds, or behaviours) the resulting music, if successful, tends to fully incorporate its other, regardless of any vocal calls to walk this or that way. Music puts things into order and provides ways of stabilising the world in terms of temporal evolution and social interaction. Musical life evolves along well-defined grids, and – notwithstanding ecstasy and freedom perceived – stays within expectable, reliable boundaries. Music is a social machine that at least apparently increases world security, stability, and confidence.

Much of musical practice that understands itself in the traditions of the European avant-garde or art music today still appears ill at ease to simply celebrate the communion of musicking.[1] At the same time it focuses its attention on structures having frequency and time relations within the defined 'musical'. I believe there is little use in fighting music's core strength: the ability to produce communion through musicking, creating a sonic sociality in music, and contend that it will always remain possible to take part in and reflect on it at once. However, music does allow for changes in positions for composer and audience alike, and makes visible or audible specific ways of mediatisation which can bring different aspects of society and the political into view and point one's ears in new, previously unheard directions.[2]

I also contend that musical composition does not need to constrain itself to the production of more works for the canons of music history, just as the reflection on and teaching of music should not be limited to the communication of recipes for how to score, produce, filter, and progress harmonically or atonally. Musical composition, practiced as an open-ended, artistic investigation, will open new vistas onto music and, in doing so, will shed new light on music's relationship to the (in)audible. Because of this it might as well and as validly lead to inaudible results, such as performative acts, objects, interventions, or specific acts of listening. And it is here that musical composition and sound art practice meet, overlap, and develop enormous potential to inform each other.

I am not proposing that it is sound art's only role to busy itself with the deconstruction of music. Even less do I want to propose a specific trajectory of progress from music into a positioning of the musical experience in sound art, and neither do I want to suggest that sound art will necessarily always be touching on the musical. Rather, at the end of my provocation I would like to suggest that extending the notion of musical composition from the fabrication of new musical pieces to a potentially unbound, aurally motivated exploration of human existence and sociality means there is no need for a clear delineation between music and sound art or, indeed, between the sonic and the (in)audible. Musical composition can and I believe should be practiced as an open-ended endeavour in a field extending over all forms of the (in)audible. This I believe provides a more promising context to compositional work than one clearly delineated as 'musical' ever could, even if it provides less of a home.

Notes

1 The term 'musicking' refers to Chris Small's book of the same name in which he makes the case that music should not be considered as thing but as an activity. Small, C. 1998. *Musicking: The Meanings of Performing and Listening*. Wesleyan University Press.

2 It is important to keep in mind that in this context 'new' never means making the 'old' obsolete, just like a newly discovered vista of a mountain peak does not render all others outdated.

Second Provocation – Cathy Lane

Why Am I a Sound Artist? Am I a Sound Artist?: some thoughts on the relationship between music and sound art

As a creative practitioner who works exclusively with sound I do not necessarily situate my own work as either music or sound art. I guess that I come from an area of art-making where any public exposure has traditionally been seen as a bonus. I don't expect to make a fortune, or sadly even a living wage from my art, so as a result, aesthetic considerations aside, I don't care whether it's exhibited as an installation or played in a concert, I'm just pleased to have the opportunity for people to hear it. I certainly don't make work that aims to plug into the gallery system or the music charts or that is designed to get me a record deal, I just kind of carry on in my own little niche happily wavering somewhere between music and sound art. I don't think about this relationship when I work, I engage in the problems of the work and how best to communicate what I'm trying to say using the techniques that I am interested in exploring. Labelling the results as music or sound art is for someone else to do.

Maybe I dissemble too much; maybe I do know the point on the continuum between music and sound art that I am working towards when I'm making a specific piece. I can feel it. To me it's something about the amount of time that I am engaging with sounding material as opposed to the amount of time that I am dealing with some kind of administrative or copyright issue or standing at the top of a ladder or running cable. The first feels 'composerly' and the others feel like working as a sound artist, and I would always prefer to be doing the first, which I guess makes me primarily a composer and puts me firmly at the music end of the continuum between them.

When then am I a sound artist?

I suppose I'm a sound artist when the work that I make seems to be outside the frame of the allowable of the music in which I 'grew up', and when the world constructed around that music only has the language and necessary references to engage a small portion of what I am trying to communicate. Music must be one of the best disciplines for gatekeeping, always seemingly safeguarding and upholding the thin idea of the possibility of pure musical discourses as layer after layer peels off and becomes rock music, world music, pop music, electroacoustic music, free music, and so on, each aligning itself with another discipline, with sociology, cultural studies, ethnography, or visual art, but somehow never quite managing a synthesis of all these inputs into something that can be taken (understood), listened to and discussed as a piece of music or 'organised sound' on its own terms.

At those times I am a sound artist, embarrassed by the narrowness of music as discussed, sometimes as played, and possibly as taught.

Equally I feel embarrassed, all too often, by the lack of sonic complexity of what is indisputably labelled as sound art, the lack of technique for dealing with sound, and the woeful underuse of its capabilities, which so often gives rise to the common joke that the trouble with sound art is that it doesn't sound very good.

As an artist I experience shades of internal difference on a work-by-work basis as to how it feels to be realising the work that I have in mind. However, the question of whether it is sound art or music never really enters my mind, nor I believe does it enter the minds of my collaborators, nor, I am very sure, any audience members or my friends who make sound work. For most artists making work the problem of classification or categorisation does not occur.

As a thinking practitioner who is employed in academia I am invited to pontificate on these problems within a given and narrow framework. But as an artist and an academic I am interested in the opening up of the sounding arts not closing possibilities down. I am interested in non-orthodoxy not new orthodoxies. If I am forced to situate my work (as the wheels of academia often force me to) I am as likely to align myself with choreographers, architects, poets, historians, or linguists as I am with those emerging from the fine arts. I am interested in shared themes and methods that traverse disciplines, areas of concern and of practice. I am not searching for new critical frameworks, I am more invested in re-investigating the existing ones to see what is interesting and relevant to the production of new sonic work. I want to work in a dynamic and free environment where sound art isn't subsumed and re-folded into music discourses or where music isn't re-discovered by the art world. I want to make work in a free and easy environment where it can be appreciated on its own terms.

Of course everything works against the realisation of my sonic utopia the minute the work leaves me and tries to find a landing place elsewhere, be it the concert hall, a gallery, a distribution company (if such things still exist), the university music department, or a new music festival. Orthodoxies exist everywhere and I have never really fitted into any of them whether it be, in my case, the pure electroacoustic community – where I cut my teeth, learned some technique, and then shied away from what I experienced as their male-centric, rarefied, technical 'whizziness', which did not relate to the world that I inhabited or wished to inhabit in my work – or the clever cerebral sound world of the white cube. That is not to say that there isn't loads of work that I love or admire in both those worlds, but for me they still do not inscribe the totality of the possibility of what sound can be, can mean and can do. I see this 'not fitting in' as a positive force and one that has driven my own work and indeed to a large extent my academic career.

What I want to see is not a further definition of categories nor indeed anything that deepens the separations between the notions of music and sound art, but a more informed approach to both, in their glorious separation by that long line of different practices.

I want to see the line broken up, to fracture and to become wide, open, and messy. I want to throw other things into the mix from other disciplines and art practices. I want an informed pluralism not an uninformed lazy dualism.

I don't want it to be neat or easy.

I want people to make an effort; for the art world to learn something of music and its discourses and languages; and for the music world to open up, relax, and accept that times they are a-changing. In fact they have changed, and thus I want music and sound art to be ever-more outward-facing and interact more with other disciplines.

I want to hear more from the practitioners themselves about their work and processes.

I want the forming of new canons to be resisted, the walls to be broken down, inclusivity and the embracing of difference.

I want multi-modality.

I want things to be judged on their own terms and not be pigeon-holed into categories set by the market or the academy.

I want us to be, as Elizabeth Grosz has suggested, 'untimely',[1] placing ourselves outside the constraints and limitations of the present to write for a future that the present cannot recognise and to develop the untimely, the out-of-place, and the out-of-step. I want us to move into a future in which the present can no longer recognise itself.

I want us all to share and learn from the bodies of knowledge that have grown up around both sound art and music practices, and to accept and open up to the huge range of diversity and variation in the rich area that can be called the sounding arts.

Notes

1 Grosz, Elizabeth. 2004. *The Nick of Time: Politics, Evolution and the Untimely*. Durham: Duke University Press. p. 117.

Transcript of Second Colloquium Discussion

Aura Satz: I would like to take Cathy's idea of 'out-of-step' and link it with Volkmar's idea of a rhythm that marches, which I found quite provocative. I wondered whether you (Volkmar) are proposing following that rhythm and being seduced by it, or whether there is any possibility of resistance from within, other than just listening?

Volkmar Klien: I don't think there is any composition that actually connects to some brain cells and makes you immediately remote-controlled. But I think music is a brilliant thing, and that the motivation behind music is that it is something that is joyful and great to do, not only in a bodily way but also on an intellectual level, in different shapes and forms and at different times. I do listen to a whole range of musics that might be incompatible, at least in terms of the guys in the Vienna Philharmonic, who hate musicians for doing other forms of music: you've got so many choices in how to behave towards the music that comes at you. Music is human interaction and you can't say how you interact with humans, that's what you do all day.

Aura: I just felt that your idea of music increasing the level of security, or wanting to take you over, or making you feel quiet and having faith in the moment—

Volkmar: But you are part of the music that takes over, if it takes over.

Aura: I feel a kind of resistance to what you are saying. There's something very problematic about it and you're not proposing it as problematic, you are putting it forward as a given, and even when you mention this idea of Germany and the masses, I just wondered if you're allowing for any resistance.

Volkmar: What I am saying is that you don't have to join in automatically. It's a choice if you are part of the music or not.

John Drever: Almost everything that has been said about music, I thought the opposite is also true: that it can repel, it can isolate, it can disgust, it can cause physical pain. Instead of all these participatory things that you are talking about, it can also completely bring one into oneself.

Helen Frosi: It is quite tribal isn't it, so if you are part of a tribe then it can be a comfortable experience.

Volkmar: It's also a tribe that you can choose. I think that's why music is so important during adolescence. People who are not musicians, who don't turn out to be musicians in the end, their musical tastes are usually set between twelve and sixteen.

Thomas Gardner: Aura, are you asking Volkmar whether, within his proposal that music produces a co-ordinated organisation of people together, there are also various ways of indicating deviation from it? For example, part of the musical content may consist of internal differences from a singular 'it', which may also be codified, but in a more obtuse and underhand way. It's got its underneath, it's got its underside, which can't be accessed in a straightforward way. And that's an interesting thing about social groups too, that it isn't simply by declaring yourself a member of a tribe that you become a member, there are underhand processes in that too.

Volkmar: Also, for the author of the music there is no position outside of the tribe, no remote control of them, you are always part of it.

Cathy Lane: Yes, if there is a tribe you want to be part of.

Volkmar: Everybody wants to be part of a tribe.

Cathy: Well, I don't know whether they do, and I don't think they should, especially if we are talking about something that is, we hope, expanding and not closing down. Surely every step in another direction, which may ultimately become a tribe, starts because people don't want to be part of the tribe they were around, that's how things progress.

Volkmar: I probably said something very different from what I wanted to say. I'm talking about a multitude of tribes that you can switch on and off, you can change from one to the other, you can make them overlap. It's like being in conversation with people.

Cathy: As I took it you gave a eulogy of music, which was great. You said some of the things that are great about music and that no one wants to lose.

Volkmar: But at the same time they are problematic. If you see a continuum into sound art you can create situations where you include changes to the listening situation as part of the artwork.

Cathy: If you think about it as a receiver then maybe you can choose what tribe you are in, but actually as a producer you would need fifty lifetimes.

Allen S. Weiss: Could I parse this out slightly differently? It sounds as if you were talking about at least two ways of being a member of such 'tribes', collectivities or communities. One of these has to do with very conscious choices: we subscribe to the opera, we go to a particular concert, we listen to a particular radio station. But, if I heard you correctly, you were speaking about something else; something that a particular piece of music does to us as we are listening and vibrating to it, which occurs in that particular instantaneous collectivity.

I am thinking, perhaps, of a slightly skewed way of looking back through the history of musicology – isn't that what *The Birth of Tragedy* was about? I keep on hearing Nietzsche in this, especially through the Austrian/German context and the difference between Dionysus and Apollo. The Dionysian is that aspect of music that gets us to dance and hum, it incorporates us, it makes us part of the music. And the Apollonian (if I'm using this language, and I know its not very precise) is the one that gives us the distance in relation to the form that permits us to choose our radio station and our opera and concert schedule for the year. They are different ways of choosing, and sometimes it's not a conscious act, but I think what you are suggesting is that 'we are chosen' by the music to become part of the collectivity, and that its not only an act of personal choice.

Volkmar: I grew up in a composition school where there was all this talk about structure, for example crystalline structures, and I strongly believe that this is a kind of faith. Part of the appeal or the power of music is that it also stops you thinking in the moment and that's not necessarily a bad thing. It's like having sex, you know, you stop thinking, and that's part of the plan, for otherwise it doesn't work.

Aura: I actually agreed with a lot of the things you suggested, it was just that I felt that a proposal of a mode of resistance didn't seem to be there.

Volkmar: But that resistance is the history of avant-garde music as told in the continental universities.

Salomé Voegelin: I am all for emotions and the pathetic to be emphasised, but I feel uneasy with the idea that we unproblematically go back to romantic collective emotionality. That led, as we said, to the huge problems of 1940s Germany, which are a consequence of that mass euphoria, and mass movement towards something. I wouldn't want to go back to that, but to something which is much more personal, and I think music can do that. Then we can share it, but I feel that that is not the bit of music heritage that I would want necessarily.

Volkmar: If you look at techno and rock concerts I think that is a given, and non-negotiable.

Nye Parry: I think there are hugely problematic things about how you can use music to manipulate large groups of people, even, for example, into buying baked beans. It plays on that aspect of music which can stop you thinking and can make you feel part of a tribe that are all buying the same baked beans. What you, Salomé, are proposing is an extremely individualistic view where you might have sympathy with how somebody else is reacting to a piece, but it excludes the communality that you get. For example, I hate Country and Western, but when I've got a mandolin in my hands and there are people playing a Country and Western song and I'm playing along, it's the best thing. It's not because I suddenly like Country and Western or feel part of that tribe, it's because I feel part of that moment, a shared form of communication that isn't linguistic and isn't verbal – that's the social aspect of music, that sense of unifying the group that you are in at that moment in time. To an extent it is about listening, but to an extent it isn't. We were talking earlier, in the break, about how kids on the bus listen to music on their iPhones without the headphones and it's just going ts ts ts ks ks ts, but because they know it's Beyoncé they are part of that group. They're not listening, it's got nothing to do with what the music sounds like that's coming out of that little machine, it's to do with that particular role of music in our society.

David Toop: How do you know what they are listening to? What gives you that special insight?

Nye: I ask them every time, and they go 'fuck off'.

Thomas: I'm thinking of the improvisation exercises John Stevens developed, which are in his book *Search and Reflect,* which are a reminder of the directness of how you perceive yourself in relation to the other people round you. It's so simple that putting it into words makes it seem more complicated. The organisation of yourself into a temporal capsule in relation to somebody else is an incredibly powerful way of experiencing yourself in a group. It involves having a rhythmic self, which you can protect and define, but which is also defined in relation to someone else's position. Both are possible, it's not either/or. It is a basic thing but it is very strange. It is an important part of music, but it is not the whole thing.

Stephen Preston: I disagree with you Thomas, I think it *is* the whole thing. The problem is that we're talking about different things, which is the enculturation of a fundamental social-biological human act. And this is the common ground, in fact. We bounce around discussing the different aspects as if they are the same thing. It's a bit like arguing whether a mouse and an elephant are both animals but we want to fix the name 'animal' to only one of them.

Allen: Somehow I agree with both of you, but I think we are talking, at the very least, about two modes or levels of time. One is the phenomenological time of the experience of the music, which is why I alluded to the Nietzsche, and Dionysus, the rhythm, which grabs you and creates that dancing collectivity. But there is also the historical time in which the music was enscribed – any work of music could be used as an example, but the one that I am thinking of since its part of the discussion about Germany is Strauss's penultimate work *Metamorphosen*, which is an elegy for a lost Germany, an elegy for the collectivity we wish hadn't existed. You can't understand the music without sensing that collectivity. About two thirds of the way in it shifts from major to minor, and it's the tragic moment and it becomes a dirge. It's very clear what it's about, and it's about a historical temporality into which we are grabbed by the musical elements of the piece.

Robert Worby: Allen, what do you mean by 'understand music'?

Allen: That at least this particular piece of music has – this is going to be delicate – 'extra-musical' implications, that is to say, it is part of a symbolic system beyond the mathematical relations between the notes.

Robert: As understood by whom, Strauss or you or anybody else?

Allen: Well what happens at this point is that we transform the colloquium into a colloquium on hermeneutics. Which might be interesting – it's a question of how one generates meaning, what one understands about symbols. One can be pretty certain about what Strauss was doing, he was writing a lament. And it's relatively hard not to hear that as a lament because one hears so much late romantic music in that piece, and then all of a sudden it becomes tragic and it's transformed into a dirge.

Robert: Doesn't it depend who is doing the listening?

Allen: Well, you know, it's interesting, because at the very beginning of our discussions the very first thing I have noted was that some of us are talking about continuum and valorising the continuum, some of us are valorising ruptures and a Foulcauldian move, and my third thing was, are we going to start talking about empiricism and pragmatism? Ultimately, if we do, we end up with that question, and then everybody is experiencing what they are experiencing and there is really no communication left and we're atomising language. I think that language works the other way. I think the fact that we need to speak about music suggests that we can answer these sorts of questions and that there are answers to them. In order to talk about any of the given pieces (I would be happier talking about *suikinkutsu* than *Metamorphosen*), I think we have to deal with two things: we have to ask the questions that you're asking, how this grabs us, which is why we bother to sit through until the end; and then we have to ask the other set of questions of why and how it was written at a particular moment in a particular place in a particular genre in relation to its history and the history of the composer. And then I think when we intersect the two we get the answer and we will escape from pure empiricism, which I don't think we want to fall into because then we would all just go home.

David: Can I ask a question to Cathy that maybe leads on from that? Cathy, when you finished your talk I just wanted to say a big YES. A couple of things stood out for me and one was that theories were out-of-date as soon as they were formulated, and the other was that you wanted less philosophers. Am I right in that you wanted less philosophy and more—

Cathy: I want to hear more from practitioners.

David: I wonder how much you feel the pressure of theory and philosophy as a force that shapes the cultural environment of sound work. It suggests maybe that you feel it as a negative influence.

Cathy: I do experience that actually, and I also feel that it's very much to do with the situation here. It's to do with the frames of reference that people bring to the table. That is why I am asking for people to take the trouble to try and learn about 'the other': if you are in music then you know about music, if you're in visual arts then you tend to know about visual arts and the gallery. Obviously I'm not saying that nobody knows about either, but I think in the academy in particular, and maybe in the gallery or the concert system, there is a tendency to stick with what you know and that acts as a gatekeeping to other things. I think it plays into all sorts of things including people that do PhD's in sound or music in a university: you're limited by the frame of reference of the team and the department around you so everything keeps on perpetuating itself.

David: At a time when there is an amazing growth of theoretical writing about sound and listening, and philosophical writing, one of the things that I feel personally is that it tends to sideline practitioners, that gradually they disappear from the discourse. I can't claim to read all of the books that come out, there are too many now, but I get to see a lot of them and gradually the practitioners disappear, and I can't see that as being a healthy trend, particularly because many of these ideas were pioneered fifty, forty, thirty years ago by practitioners when theorists/philosophers weren't interested. The groundwork was done by people with their hands in the mud, as it were.

Cathy: I totally agree. I think that the other thing within sound discourse, and I have to align myself a little bit with Salomé and

Volkmar, is that sound art is relatively ignorant about musicological discourses. I don't know so much about the other way around, but I think that there is a lot that musicology and music theory of all sorts has to offer that is very hidden, and I don't know if that's because music departments in academies don't open out and do anything to widen the appeal, whether they stick very much to the music gang, and don't go out with the other gangs enough.

Claudia Molitor: I don't know whether it has anything to do with what you were saying David. The difficulty with music, when you are talking about composition, is that you are not really writing music, you are sort of making it, but you are not really making anything concrete: that's why we are all obsessed with stationary because that's the only thing that we make, paper and pen. But in the art world we've got an object, we make something and then we can look at that object or installation or painting and we can always return back to it and go, ok this was made and we can see how it was made. In music that is much more difficult to hold onto because there is no made object and maybe that's why it becomes so important that you go back to the people that have either written the score or have played from the score or have improvised on their instrument and actually talk to them about the motivations.

Angus Carlyle: I'd be worried about fetishising this notion of manufacture. David was talking about the practitioner with their hands in the mud, but there can also be a practitioner with their ears in the mud too. And I think that the philosopher does not need to be someone who dirtied themselves with pens and papers and music, and to be someone for whom practice and the heard world is an inspiration to their engagement with it. I'd be careful about isolating this moment of genius in the compositional creativity.

Claudia: But when writing something down, everything goes on in the head.

Angus: It does and doesn't, there are lots of different levels of engagement that are happening. Some of those levels are ones that are intriguing, as much from the point of view of the listener as from the composer, whose intentionality you want to focus on and explore. I would be careful about finding in that moment of dirty-handed genius the only thing.

David: She never said that!

Justin Yang: Can I offer a bit of a connection? One the things the sound art world brings is another kind of participation, which puts the shoe on the other foot. So we have seminal composers, for example Alvin Lucier, who refocus the compositional effort away from the creator and towards the listener. So a piece like *Music on a Long Thin Wire,* depending on where you are in the room, on your own physiology, is created with your body. A fair amount of the sound art I've experienced does delve into that area, where the boundary between the creator, sound image and the received image is part of the compositional aspect of the piece. Maybe it joins with what Volkmar was saying, but is a kinder model. Rather than have this vociferous music that takes over your mind, perhaps there is another model of music that we create with our minds. That we participate in as a co-creator.

Volkmar: Reading a book is allowing somebody else to take over your mind for the time you are reading it, in a certain way.

Salomé: Reading is not like taking a drug, it's an effort of interpretation. It's a participation in the writing.

Volkmar: The semantics of music is something I worry about.

Does it mean stuff or does it do stuff? A word means something in a different way that alcohol does stuff.

Allen: It should be clear, you're making an inclusive disjunction and not an exclusive disjunction when you say that, or at least I think you should be!

Volkmar: Meaning?

Allen: Meaning exactly what's being said on the other side of the table, that it is doing both at the same time, but you could distinguish between the operations.

Cathy: I'd like to jump into what you said Justin, because I think that what you said is true to some extent, but I think it also represents what is becoming the public face of those two sides: that music is the thing that we all think of as participatory and tribal, and sound art is something that allows us to participate in a different way and its relatively cerebral. I am trying to argue against those two oppositions and I want to fill the space in-between. What is happening is that people identify music and put it in a concert hall, and they identify sound art and it goes into a gallery, but what about all the fantastic stuff that isn't either of them?

Justin: Well, forgive me again for throwing a theory into this, but what I think is presented in the Lucier model is a Lyotardian multiple discourse, multiple narrative. It's a different model: we are part of the whole and at the same time you have a bit of very individual experience. I don't know if that is a cheat utopia. I do hope that it does enter into another generational way of listening.

Allen: Part of the question goes back to the reading of the model as score. Perhaps statistically that is not the case around this table, but probably the majority of people listening to sound art in galleries, or wherever, are 'textually literate', and probably the great majority of them are not what we used to call 'musically literate', that is to say they can't read a score and they can't play an instrument. In terms of the question of the intellectual side or cognitive side (I don't know what words to use, so many have been going around the table) it seems to me that this question of literacy has something to do with the types of experience that we could expect, and the types of discourses that could be generated. It also might in part explain what I am beginning to hear as a rift between a discourse on sound art and a discourse on music. Many people might feel they have more access to a discourse on sound art because they are not lacking the musical literacy that would be needed for an adequate discourse about music.

Cathy: Yes, I totally agree with that. I think there is a rift. I took that as a given. I presumed that I was in a room of people that felt that rift. I don't think it works only one way, it's both ways. I think that people who come from a very musical background feel a lack as well, they don't have access to a long history of the kind of philosophical engagement and conceptual engagement that might come with a more visual arts, liberal arts background.

Robert: That may come, as music lags behind the other arts by at least fifty years. Picking up David's philosopher/practitioner distinction, if we go back to the 1950s the modernist composers like Stockhausen, Xenakis, Cage all wrote about their practice, they wrote books about it. But Jackson Pollock didn't write a book, Clement Greenberg wrote a book. Jasper Johns didn't write a book, Robert Rauschenberg didn't write a book about what they did, and Clement Greenberg was the person who wrote about painting and changed our way of thinking about painting and what those paintings meant and what they were. But

Stockhausen wrote the music and told us how he wrote it, and so did Cage. The composers wrote about it and told us what they did.

Leigh Landy: Which brings us to a point that has been mentioned by various people in different ways. Giuseppe di Giugno, the guy that made the 4x computer for IRCAM, once said to me, 'I think music has to find a place between the heart and the mind', and then he went on to tell an anecdote which I'll repeat: 'I've been working with these two guys for a long time, one's called Berio and the other's called Boulez and the problem is that I think Berio wants to be loved so he is using too much of the heart, but Boulez I can assure you, its all coming from the head.' He had just heard a concert that worked somewhere in the middle, or combined it in different proportions in different pieces. 'I just heard that combination, I know it's possible, why aren't people doing this!' and so when we start challenging 'what does understanding mean', or we want the practitioners to talk, talk about what?

Cathy, I know, would not write 100 pages about the formalism in her compositions that leads to the following application of fractal theory, she would talk about something that would also involve the heart, thank God! I have the Stockhausen books, but he never discussed the listening experience, the contextual experience, and God forbid the emotional experience. John Cage hints at it, bless his soul, but does not go there either. Because the discourse of the time was actually 'up here'. As an American-born, I read those dissertations by the composers, all of whom quantified their compositions, because that is easier to write about, and they all sounded like 'bull****' (I will leave the word to the side) in general, because they hadn't addressed this axis. You are all talking about the same thing, and it's finding that position in the tribes, communities, collectives, or whatever they are called. There's an intellectual understanding, there's an emotional communication. Aesthetics went from an emotional given to an intellectual given for 150 years, and it's now completely lost. And I think Salomé and Thomas have asked people to come together to find out where, along this axis you propose from music to sound art, we can find this other axis. It has to address these understandings as well, and if we can get to that, we'll get somewhere.

Simon Emmerson: May I pick up on the tribalism that Leigh and everybody else has mentioned. I thought that the idea of tribalism coming together with Volkmar's use of the word 'faith' reminded me of ghastly parallels. The dark side is always with us… one was Xenakis's being in Athens during the occupation as a member of the resistance, and his description of finding machine guns as a statistical sound world, which is actually quite horrendous if you think about it. Also, from that generation, Karlheinz Stockhausen describing 9/11 as Lucifer's greatest work of art. Of course he was pilloried in the press, but there is a ghastly truth about that phrase if it was really understood in its context. The dark side is always there, it's simply the other side of the coin and we won't be able to avoid it. There was a fascinating paper saying that Xenakis was going to do Polytopes in Berlin but the sketches for it involved aircraft, high-powered lights and the like, and it looked too much like 1937 and it was neatly lost in the Berlin commissioning system. So these things are all there, and they have all the possibilities of one side or another of the word 'tribe'.

Responses

Abstracts

Leigh Landy

My text is largely based on a reaction to remarks presented during the colloquium, in particular the introductory speakers' arguments in the session to which I was asked to respond. I knew that I wanted to address the point summarised in the subtitle to my text, 'finding value for the heart *and* the brain', and also to see to what extent sound art and electroacoustic music's artistic manifestations and related scholarship could be not only drawn together, but also form new synergies. In my writing I suggest that we focus on three important words: experience, expectation, and change. Beyond this, the points made were spontaneously formed as responses to the excellent food for thought provided by all present.

Aura Satz

For her response to the colloquium Aura Satz was in conversation with Thomas Gardner about the selected elements of the transcription that focus primarily on the tribal, marching, and the collective rhythms proposed in Klien's provocation.

'I want to problematise what draws me to music, lures me into it whilst also repelling me. I am profoundly interested in the immersive quality of the perceptual, be it visual or auditory. This quality is something I return to time and again in my own work and research interests. I tend to be drawn to hypnotic qualities, visual and acoustic patterning which, through its very nature, suck us in and allow us to lose our sense of boundary. There is a certain positive ideological loosening that comes from becoming uncertain of one's sense of self, a potential questioning which might not lead to a pre-determined answer. That said, one must be aware that these same strategies of seductive relief and release are problematic, if harnessed for the wrong purposes. I suppose my main interest is in agency, how one can remove a certain fixity or stability of the body, how it can be challenged through perception into a new understanding of itself, whilst at the same time be awakened into a critical awareness of the very mechanisms at play. How can one be both sucked in and spewed out of an immersive experience, perceptually allured, lulled, entranced, or assaulted, and at the same time engaged in a heightened sense of awareness. And what is offered by such an experience, that is both somewhat unmediated, or uncritical as a first-hand sensory encounter, but gradually emerges as critically vital and agitating.'

First Response – Leigh Landy

Sound Art 'vs' Electroacoustic Music: finding value for the heart **and** *the brain*

1. Two of the introductory 'provocations' at the colloquium as point of departure

Listening to Salomé Voegelin's introductory provocation in the previous session, I heard thoughts expressed for the first time, which I believe were articulating a long-standing frustration I had experienced regarding the perceived space between sound art and electroacoustic music, my own field and the main subject of the following pages. Salomé's point relating to sound artists' focus on concept and context and musicians' on listening, when taken a step further, implied to me that both sound artists and electroacoustic musicians were missing some things that they could learn from one another. As this was a provocation, I took Salomé's thoughts as rhetorical extremes. Of course, all artists, regardless of art form, deal with concept, not least musicians. And there are musicians more interested in musical construction than listening, for better or, often, for worse.

So allow me to reword her thoughts for the benefit of this reaction. In the case of sound artists, there exists an array of highly developed electroacoustic composition and manipulation techniques that sometimes appear to be glossed over in sound art works. (This has led some to consider sound art as poor electroacoustic music, a very significant error in my view, as it misses the *raison d'être* of sound art.) Furthermore, as Salomé clearly stated, the approaches to analytical discourse within sound art usually rely heavily on those from the visual arts not those normally associated with music, thus not focusing on the above-mentioned aspects of sonic construction. Conversely, electroacoustic musicians could learn about the link with place, time, in short context, which is often a key conceptual focus of a sound art work, in terms of construction, reception, and analysis. This important thought has profound consequences as it brings us to the heart of why contemporary music from the early 20th century onwards has been far less appreciated than it could and maybe should have been. I am therefore grateful to Salomé for this view. I, too, had previously tackled part of the issue of perceived distance between sound art and electroacoustic music in a discussion in *Understanding the Art of Sound Organization* (2007)[1] in which I coined a new term, *sound-based music*, which was intended to bring together a very significant portion of electroacoustic music and sound art, not to mention sonic art, electronica and so on, thus the 'vs' in the title within inverted commas. With this term I am seeking not only clarity but also a type of synthesis between overlapping terms dealing with sound organisation. I understand Salomé to be seeking a type of synthesis, something I also attempted with the creation of that new term.

In relation to this, Volkmar Klien's provocation at the start of this session and further discussed by Thomas Gardner (and others) offered interesting views regarding the notion of new tribes or communities developing as these new forms of art evolve. The socio-cultural aspect of innovative art is certainly deserving of greater attention, not least in our networked information age. What is it that forms these ephemeral collectives and how do they, if they do this at all, create value systems related to experiences of these innovative, primarily aural, art forms? In other words, what are the criteria of choice concerning these groups' and individuals' tastes as related to innovative sonic practice?

We shall return to both of these points in the following sections.

2. Three words

In one of my interventions during this fascinating colloquium, I suggested that we focus on three important words: *experience*, *expectation*, and *change*. The most important word of the three regarding these discussions was the first one, *experience*. Let me put it this way: only the most open of minds is willing to place a high value on an artistic experience that in no way relates to that individual's expectations and is solely valued on the basis of its radical change. In other words, we normally do not have the capacity to place a value on new aspects of our lives *ex nihilo*. We generally link something new, whether it is to do with knowledge, food, or art, with something that we have experienced and, where relevant, compare this to expectations we have developed through our experience base. It is only then that change can be valued.

It is clear that both art forms, sound art and electroacoustic music, if we choose to separate them, are founded on experimentation and innovation, thus change. Some of these changes have been truly revolutionary, some more evolutionary, and as both art forms mature it has become apparent that some are not that innovative at all. For example, there are many sonic clichés that can be discovered in an expanding number of electroacoustic works. These clichés are an acknowledgement and sign perhaps of successful formulae, but they are also a bit of a challenge to the idea of electroacoustic music as an innovative arts medium.

What is important here is whether constant change serves our art or whether expectation – in whatever relevant form – is needed to allow listeners to have some things to hold onto in their listening experience. It is here where I suggest that innovative arts will normally not succeed unless they allow for some form of experiential link, ideally including an aspect of expectation alongside elements of surprise.

I have often noticed that people of all ages, but in particular young people, when encountering something new in art, for example, an abstract-expressionist painting, seek something that they can connect with. In the case of Jackson Pollock, realistic objects are sometimes 'identified' in a painting that is more about action than content. Only after becoming acquainted with many manifestations of abstract expressionism can foundations for discussion be discovered and, ideally, systems of value developed. (I shall discuss the notion of value in the following section.)

Even from the standpoint of experimental artistic production, one notices how performers can create expectations. For example, I have heard many similar concerts of free jazz raising the question how free 'free' is. It is true that I have also heard some very wild improvisations where almost no link can be made with either free jazz conventions or with any other musical genre; however, that is the exception not the rule. Similarly, I have witnessed many performances and heard many recordings of, for example, Earle Brown's early graphic pieces that sound alike: dissonant, involving little to no beat, focusing on extended instrumental techniques, and so on. The graphic in no way implies this, but people create expectations related to the musical context of the time.

So let's look at those three words, experience, expectation, and change, with regard to listeners outside of the specialist community. A recording of an Anton Webern instrumental work or an electroacoustic piece by Iannis Xenakis is so distant from most listeners' lived experience that the only elements to hold onto are novelty and the lack of tools to navigate the work. Someone not that knowledgeable of Gustav Mahler in the late 19th/early 20th century would not have confronted such problems, as the majority of Mahler's work fell within the known and involved certain elements of expectation. By contrast, Arnold Schönberg may have dreamt of our whistling his twelve-tone rows, but it is only the specialist listener who can truly 'understand' radical, antithetical change and develop forms of musical expectation.

As someone obsessed with making innovative art accessible

to a more optimally sized public than is currently the case, I believe that part of the role of the sonic artist is to take these three words into account in order to aid community forming and the development of value systems. If we ignore these issues, marginalisation for many of us electroacoustic musicians will continue.

So the question must be raised: why is marginalisation not as relevant to sound artists? The annual Turner Prize shortlist seems to include at least one sound artist these days, which certainly does not suggest marginalisation. In my opinion the answer to this reception gap has to do with three things: 1) the art world, in particular that of painting and sculpture, has attracted a much larger audience than new music has, perhaps because much of it is not time-based. One can observe a work for as long or short as one wants. This is largely due to the fact that 2) much visual art has succeeded in dealing with the three words, despite the spikes of radical change that have been introduced from time to time over the last hundred-plus years. And 3) yes, this artistic area is related to the visual, and the notion of 'visual culture' is alive and well today.

Returning to Salomé's point, and in answer to Cathy Lane's provocation staged at the beginning of this session, focusing on applying a concept to a specific situation, sound art is largely context related. People have an idea of who their audience, large or small, may be due to where the work is shared or what it is based upon. By contrast, the elitist, although perhaps not originally intended to be so, notion of art for art's sake allows new musicians the freedom to share little about their work and not to be interested in specific aspects of reception. If reception is of little to no interest, then so is expectation and perhaps even experience; and change *an sich* is not what makes art good, at least in my view. It *is* what makes art, and, to an extent, society, both move forward but change is a vital tool, not a driving force.

3. The heart *and* the brain

The word, 'value' has been showing its face in this short tale from time to time. It is a term that can be used comfortably when people carefully avoid discussing aesthetics. However, value can have several meanings. This is not the place to rehearse the diversity of meanings, so only two will be presented, one related to emotion and the other to what might be called understanding.

Although some readers may have heard the following anecdote from me before, I would like to share the nicest brief remark on aesthetics that I have ever heard, which I shall now paraphrase. It was the physicist/technologist Giuseppe di Giugno who, after a concert at Bretton Hall where I was working at the time, shared it with me, saying the following:

> You know I've worked closely with two composers at IRCAM in recent years, Pierre Boulez and Luciano Berio. Boulez composes for the brain, but Berio wants to be loved, so he composes for the heart [a bit of an exaggeration, in my opinion, but his point was taken]. I [Di Giugno] have always believed that contemporary music should address both the heart and the brain and the concert I just heard demonstrates this. Many thanks.

This short remark summarises the history of aesthetics eloquently. Originally, one valued the artistic experience primarily from the point of view of the intensification of experience, e.g. pleasure. Subsequently, approximately two centuries ago, aesthetics drifted away from the emotional and more towards the intellectual, focusing on the language of construction, on, for example, what many philosophers called 'absolute music' (whether of that era or any other) that was not *about* anything. Listeners were expected to 'feel theory'; in other words, understand the art of musical construction. As said earlier, a Mahler piece may also not necessarily be about anything in particular, but its language included much that was known. Therefore, absolute or not, it allowed those with the greatest theoretical knowledge to feel the music's theory, but less specialist listeners to simply enjoy an intensified experience.

Modernist 20th-century composers rarely engaged with discussions regarding the heart/brain divide, or however one calls it, largely focusing on the cerebral: their musical language and the absolute. I have often discovered that I have not been emotionally engaged by such pieces; rather, the key intensification of experience was my attempt to solve the composer's puzzle.

Algorithmic composers and others favouring some form of formalisation from the second Viennese School by way of Xenakis and Stockhausen and many others more recently rarely seem to take the emotional experience into account. It is *not* impossible, but simply not their key concern. Note: some sound artists who, for example, seek simple sonification of a given aspect of daily life can also get locked into formal sonic translation above any concern for the listening experience, so this focus on one type of value is not only relevant to those within music, as it appears to be true in all art forms.

Di Giugno proposes a sliding scale, as do I, and the avoidance of the two poles: *brain <–> heart* or *just understanding <–> just feeling*. With this in mind, I propose the following title for the final part of this discussion:

4. After thesis and antithesis comes synthesis, if things go well, doesn't it?

When I was a student of composition in the 1970s, I was more or less obligated to compose post-serial music at my university. This approach focused on the formalisation of construction and was based, often exclusively, on dissonant sonorities. It did not correspond with my evolving more eclectic musical vision, one that allows for formal construction and dissonance, but also one where the final aesthetic judge is the ear, not the method. Being an atonal composer was a stance, at least at that time. It had its own international tribe in the sense referred to by Volkmar and Thomas. The tribe in question was the group of composers making this type of music and very few others. Its audience was, in my view, insular, as the tribe in terms of reception was almost identical to the tribe of its creation. If that had been the goal, there would be no need to criticise it, but that was not the case. The perceived importance emanating from its makers did not correspond with reception. This contradiction led me to spend a quarter-century investigating innovative music and issues related to its accessibility beyond its specialist audience where construction, intention, context, and reception all play an important role.

My discovery after this lengthy search is summarised by what has been presented above. Innovative sound art and electroacoustic (or sound-based) music will only resonate when it somehow optimises the combination of experience, expectation, and change thus synthesising thesis (the intensification of experience) and antithesis (absolute music or art/feeling theory). Without the latter, focusing on construction and change, we stagnate; without the first, we become marginalised.

One question rarely posed in the contemporary arts, in particular music, is *for whom* a given work is being made. Part of my means of optimisation is the (sometimes tedious) creation of flexible works; that is, works made to optimise linking novelty with making bridges with lived experience providing a particular community of listeners with things to hold onto so that their expectation is never neglected.

Sound artists have thrived in general at offering those connections with diverse audiences, as suggested in this text's introductory remarks, regarding art and context of presentation. Electroacoustic musicians, on the other hand, have often primarily tackled the very challenging issue of infinite material and structure, thus reflecting a focus on musical construction. I would suggest that if we are to optimise our audiences, we should also optimise our sharing of good practice across the spectrum of artistic forms of sound organisation.

In my 2007 book, I proposed that there exists a sound-based music paradigm, one that, for example, lives outside of established norms such as art and popular musics, music and visual art. This world of sound-based music allows people with dissimilar sonic visions to create a vast space, one in which many communities of interest can exist. Fortunately these communities overlap a great deal, allowing our vast area to be highly dynamic.

I hope, therefore, that such communities can flourish in spite of our age of visual and celebrity cultures. Electroacoustic composers would then take the context of reception more into account and sound artists could enrich their palette of techniques of construction and the tribe can, in consequence, discuss both the poetic language of creation as well as the intensified experience of reception.

Notes

1 Landy, L. 2007. *Understanding the Art of Sound Organisation*. Cambridge, Mass.: MIT Press.

Second Response – Aura Satz

Out of Step / A Rhythm that Marches: Aura Satz in conversation with Thomas Gardner

Thomas Gardner: In the second session of the colloquium there was a recurrent focus on the tribal, almost unthinking collectivity which music can enable. Your question – 'is there any possibility of resistance from "within" music?' – opens up a really important swathe of ideas. Part of the background discussion related to the aftermath of the German Nazi period, and the continental avant-garde's consequent distrust of musical participation (hence an increased emphasis on the 'listener'). A further background was your own observation of the complex synchronisation between the visible and the audible. Although these are difficult waters, I felt it would be extremely valuable to explore them further, and would like to invite you to do so, taking in any discussion which you find relevant elsewhere in the colloquium.

Aura Satz: I want to problematise what draws me to music, lures me into it whilst also repelling me. I am profoundly interested in the immersive quality of the perceptual, be it visual or auditory. This quality is something I return to time and again in my own work and research interests. I tend to be drawn to hypnotic qualities, visual and acoustic patterning which, through their very nature, suck us in and allow us to lose our sense of boundary. There is a certain positive ideological loosening that comes from becoming uncertain of one's sense of self, a potential questioning which might not lead to a pre-determined answer. That said, one must be aware that these same strategies of seductive relief and release are problematic, if harnessed for the wrong purposes. I suppose my main interest is in agency, how one can remove a certain fixity or stability of the body, how it can be challenged through perception into a new understanding of itself, whilst at the same time be awakened into a critical awareness of the very mechanisms at play. And so the varied strategies of an aesthetic experience and the way they enable or arouse a certain type of listening or spectatorship is at the core of my thinking. How can an aesthetic experience both determine one's response, whilst allowing for the possibility of resistance from within? How can one be both sucked in and spewed out of an immersive experience, perceptually allured, lulled, entranced, or assaulted, and at the same time engaged in a heightened sense of awareness? And what is offered by such an experience, that is both somewhat unmediated, or uncritical as a first-hand sensory encounter, but gradually emerges as critically vital and agitating?

Thomas: Thank you very much for this cogent outline of your perspective.

To begin our conversation I would like to revisit the discussion in the colloquium, which considered the place occupied by German music in the aftermath of the Second World War. In particular, I want to ask your opinion on the difference between the post-war music of the Darmstadt School and the approach taken by John Cage and Fluxus artists. The Darmstadt School of New Music, with its rejection of uncritical musical enjoyment, is linked to Cage in many ways (the Boulez–Cage correspondence has fantastic detail), for example in its avoidance of tonal rhetoric, exploration of the role of chance, and a distancing from habitual musical forms. However, a difference between them could be seen in the place occupied by stress, pain, and rigour. The intellectual energy of Darmstadt had a lot to do with pain, with, as it were, recognising and responding to the cataclysms unleashed during the war – whether containing, atoning for, or finding a less sullied discourse. A flavour that is, on the surface, very different from that of Cage, Fluxus, and Zen.

So, for my first question, I'd like to ask you if there is anything in your artistic practice that connects you to work that was going on in Europe and America in the '50s, or if you see any important distinctions between them?

As an addendum I want to evoke the spectre of Eugen Gomringer's work *Ping Pong* from 1953, to reflect the possibility of our conversation.

Aura: Strangely I would say that many of my artistic references are actually from a much earlier period. I was fascinated for many years by early Byzantine art and the consequent iconoclastic clashes that emerged and created a discursive forum for early image theory. Although this moves away from music and sound art I think it is still relevant and I also read it into my more contemporary points of reference. The 6th century was awash with the cult of images and icons, relics, *acheiropoieta* (images not made by human hands), and the miraculous inanimate was out of control, in the sense that the Church lost its hold over these powerful portals for the general public. Those that reacted against the proliferation of icons reacted against visual pleasure, facile sensual engagement, fearing that it would lead to an art of excessive luxury and corrupting material seduction. Accounts of miraculously formed images, not made by human hands, produced automatically as traces, relics, or miraculous paintings, led me to ponder on what the actual destruction of a material object might produce, what happens to belief, how might materiality and a different sensory 'way in' shift a perceptual paradigm.

My interest in sound and particularly sound reproduction technology stems directly from this fascination with trace-making techniques and automatic image production. For me the phonograph is very much part of the same lineage of *acheiropoieta*, a method of automatic writing whereby the stylus writes the voice without human hands. Likewise my interest in the removal of authorship, the use of aleatory means for music composition, is also aligned with this drive towards the removal of human agency, or at least the questioning of authorship, ownership, intention, to allow new meanings to emerge. An image or sound that survives in material form (recording, notation, etc.) but somehow resists or subverts its own materiality, marks an opening in how it is then read and interpreted. I have always been very much taken by Brechtian distancing or the alienation effect, which I think provides a good example of resistance from the inside, through an iconoclastic stance against illusion. The performance intends for the audience to be 'hindered from simply identifying itself with the characters in the play' (Brecht, 1936)[1], unable to empathise emotionally or lose themselves in the sensual pleasure of merely watching in a passive way. One way of providing resistance from within is creating constant reminders of the fact that you are watching a construct, being made aware of its manipulative contrivances, catching yourself in the act of perceiving and therefore retaining a heightened sense of attention. Similarly, I am attracted to music or sound materials that draw attention to their own making, their material and/or technological support mechanism, and the complexity of the source of sound, its authorship. As you rightly point out, all of these are intensely flavoured by pre-war, war and post-war revisions to what it means to write, document, record, listen, spectate, observe, and actually have a voice, alongside the drastic technological shifts that were occurring at the same time, most notably radio and magnetic tape (technologies of voice dissemination, alienation from the source, propaganda, as well as dissection, destruction, censorship, etc.).

In discussing Gomringer's *Ping Pong* what I find most interesting is precisely the opening of a singular voice to a syncopated racket of back-and-forth, between alternating states (being both sucked in and spewed out, losing oneself and finding oneself).

And more crucially, the notion that in breaking the unity of the voice, creating an audible crack, so to speak, other voices are allowed in.

I've not really touched upon the question of rhythm, which is a really key aspect to what we were discussing at the colloquium. But perhaps again this can be related to the notion of how you are sucked in, in an almost Fordian way, to a certain repetitive pace, enslaved to the rhythm. But when rhythm is broken down, or aspects of its own construction become apparent (as with Steve Reich's phasing technique or certain Structuralist film practices) and small cracks enable a more attentive mode of listening in which you simply cannot be a slave to the rhythm because it is constantly breaking apart.

Thomas: It's very interesting that you mention the Byzantine clashes around the use of icons and iconic imagery, and link this to our current discussion about sound and music.

I suppose one aspect of this is that the 'icon' refers to some kind of miraculous wholeness, whose authorship may be open to interpretation but whose compelling and talismanic properties are not to be denied. And whilst music is able to sidestep the question of whether it is an icon of something else, it nonetheless, in this absence of tangible representation, holds out an even more dangerous promise, which is that it is somehow something 'in itself', not even an icon, but the actual thing.

Our seduction by this, and our inability to objectify or defend against it, was linked (in the colloquium) to a danger of unthinking tribalism.

Your question of the potential for a 'resistance from within' seemed particularly right. The strategies that you mention, of Brechtian distancing, a consciousness of the manipulative contrivances, or of a deliberate allowing-in of 'automatic writing' coming from diverse technologies, all seem to be ways of opening and diversifying the seduction, but also still seem to be placed in some way 'outside' of music. This seems interesting, as the notion that there is an 'inside' or some kind of central content of music is, perhaps, a reversion to religious thinking.

I have several questions that come from this:

The first is to ask for your thoughts on 'measurement', which is perhaps my own defence against religious thinking. In particular, that musical forms of measure do have a resistance to any simple reduction. Thus, both in the measure of musical time and pitch space, there are apparently incompatible forms of measurement. There is the metronomic repetitive pace that you mention, which is derived from an external measure of duration, allowing a certain kind of equality of comparison between different moments of time; but there is also the unavoidable inner human perspective of duration, which is an accelerating curve as time passes and one gets older (i.e. The first year of your life is an infinitely longer time than the fortieth year). Thus, these two perspectives of time, both of which are perceptually very simple, are also 'resistant' to absorption by the other and do not lead to a simple resolution. This is also true in pitch space, where the overtone series provides a hierarchical set of relationships between pitches, whilst the simple question of 'what is halfway between one pitch and another?' provides a more democratic and external form of measure. To me, this provides a partial answer to the question of resistance from within, in that our musical engagement has to act with these apparently incommensurable forms of measure – thus creating a situation that gives rise to a diversity of understandings, and leads us to draw on and find the enabling support of apparently contradictory modes of perception, a process giving rise to tact, sensitivity, and culture.

Aura: It's really fascinating that you have brought in the concept of measure, as this is something I am obsessed with at the moment, though not so much explicitly in relation to music. I have been looking at women's contributions to astronomy and ballistics, and in particular their painstaking perceptual efforts to measure distance, calibrate a sense of scale (the distance of earth to a certain galaxy), or the speed at which a bullet travels from gun barrel to target. I would like to introduce here the concept of interpolation, as I have been grappling with this in my film *Between the Bullet and the Hole*. Mathematically, interpolation is a method of constructing new data points within the range of a discrete set of known data points, but perhaps we can bring this back into the discussion – musical interpolation is the insertion of an abrupt change in the middle of a phrase (I am thinking for example of Krzysztof Penderecki's *Threnody for the Victims of Hiroshima*). Two slightly different strategies of interpolation: fill in the gaps, calculate the spaces in-between, draw hypothetical continuities, or, on the contrary, generate a rift, a decisive break or discontinuity, an abrasive interruption. Ultimately I am more interested in ways in which we can upset the measure, or at least question it, interrupt it so it becomes unsettled and variable. A regular measure seems to suggest a fixed sense of scale, of time, of experience, and one which we can succumb to quite easily. A disruption in the measure reconfigures experience as it requires a heightened state of attention.

In my film projects I am always keen to try to stretch the space between sound and image, to see how far apart they can be pulled before they lapse back into one another, find a rhythmic counterpart in visual or sonic sequences. I started off with an interest in sound-visualisation technologies that seemed to enable perfect synchronisation, but this actually led to a greater investment in asynchrony. I try to use the image to offset the sound, and vice versa, in order to generate a productive tension between the two, so that the image makes you listen differently just as the sound shifts your visual perception. The 'resistance' is therefore somehow embedded rhythmically, in pattern changes, ruptures, and gaps that allow for something else to emerge. It can be the dislocated space between the sound and image, or a blank screen, an awkward silence, or a friction that is too dense to apprehend. I have long been fascinated by the use of flicker in the films of Tony Conrad and Paul Sharits, both working with film frames that vary in pulse; sometimes it's a strobe, other times it's a throbbing, and at other times it assaults the senses to create neurological after-images. Although filmic it is also inherently musical and by playing with the frame rate something is activated, we are drawn to the flicker whilst also being expelled by it.

Thomas: Thank you very much for that. I am delighted that you are also finding this question of measurement to be something meaningful in your work. Your notion of 'interpolation' feels like a very productive way of thinking about it. Perhaps the quality or meaning of the act of interpolation is something we could discuss further.

You already mentioned the disruptive kinds of interpolation, where a rhythm is broken down, or a seemingly fixed form of measurement is opened up, and these were linked to real-world issues of hierarchy and equality, responding to the injustice of overlooked or unheard women scientists and artists.

It seems that in making this linkage between the more apparently 'in-vitro' musical interpolations of hierarchy and equality, and the hidden processes of valuation and judgement that influence our everyday life, that you are doing something quite specific – bringing perceptible processes of measurement to our attention within the artwork, and simultaneously engaging with imbalances, lacks, and latent potentials in our everyday world. Also, that this, by definition, also includes the interpolation between seeing and hearing, and the artistic practices within which they might operate.

Your exploration of women's research into ballistics is a case in point. The physical 'facts' of the ballistics of sound or movement blend with and are enabled by a culturally constructed awareness. In a similar way, I have been very interested in the differences between Baroque constructions of musical space and 19th-century ones. Certain kinds of ballistics become culturally overlooked or unheard, for example the Baroque use of reverberation and echo in the space was gradually replaced by an interest in more continuous and saturating sound production (for example vibrato). Certain kinds of interpolation seem unimaginable, and realising these, either rediscovering or inventing them, is a source both of pleasure and justice.

I wondered, in relation to this, what you feel about a different, more apparently idealistic direction in which these interpolations may take us. My particular pleasure in experiencing the opening up of relations between hierarchical and democratic structures in musical works has a distinctly non-worldly side to it. It is as if the specific techniques point to an unlimited capacity to bring happiness. If the particular ways in which the techniques liberate us from dominance and oversimplification could be applied universally, then any particular 'musical' in-vitro experience could be proof of the possibility of an ideal world. Perhaps the best thing is that each experience at least gives a sense of hope, and that specific interpolation techniques do have actual applicability and critical purchase?

Aura: I'm intrigued by your reference to pleasure and justice. I hadn't necessarily thought of the opening or unsettling of hierarchical structures in relation to justice. I do think throughout this conversation we have been touching upon strategies of resistance, iconoclasm, and disruption (to authorship, a dictatorial rhythm, a regular measure). I quite like this idea of pleasure and justice being linked, though I also distrust it. In setting up some kind of internal disturbance of measurement I'm not quite sure I want to replace it with an alternative canon. If anything, what I seem to come back to again and again is the possibility of productively inhabiting this space of disruption, allowing it to exist rather than trying to smooth it over. Like you, I am keen to address gaps in history, to look at the overlooked and make audible the unheard. As such I feel a certain responsibility to my subject matter and a profound investment in the methods of perception used to approach these. But I am not sure this points to an idealism... If anything I would return to the notion of a heightened mode of attention, an acute state of focus, which I like to both represent (for example women engaged in focused research and small perceptual acts) as well as re-enact. To me attention is what has critical purchase – the ability of something, a sound or an image, to perturb apathy and distraction and provoke concentration. Attention as in attending to, tending to, close looking or listening, tension, stretching or reaching towards. This is my creative strategy, often I use close-up in my camera work, and the role of the lens, magnifying glass or microscope runs parallel my interest in amplification devices such as horns and hearing aids, the attempt to draw out small sounds or voices that have been unheard. I'm not sure if this sets out a new measurement or simply interpolates smaller units, opens up what can be measured, who is doing the measuring, and where one might position oneself in relation to the scale.

Thomas: That's a wonderfully rich and detailed response. I was struck by the connection between 'interpolation' and the heightened attention that you describe. The moment of interpolation results from awareness of different kinds of measurement, whilst simultaneously deriving a point of cohabitation. The attention is discursive, in that it responds to the structuring of incommensurable ways of measuring, but it is also focused in that it results in the creative construction of a particular point or place in time. As you say, it's very different from distraction or boredom, and also very different from being uncritically carried away by a single focus or ideal.

I feel that we should bring our ping-pong dialogue to a close at this point, in order to allow this moment to reverberate a little longer. I'm very grateful that we have been able to explore in a little more depth what this 'resistance from within' might entail, and also to have come upon the chance discovery that measurement, for both of us, has a place within this resistance.

Notes

1 Brecht, Bertolt. 2005. 'Alienation Effects in Chinese Acting' (1936). In D. Johnson (ed.), *A Twentieth-century Literature Reader: Texts and Debates*. Psychology Press.

PART THREE:
Participation, Listening, and Place

Provocations

Abstracts

Simon Emmerson

Many forms of 'sound art' do not 'begin and end' so much as 'start and stop' (cf. Stockhausen's description of 'moment form') as defined by a probably ambulant listener – creating a potentially much greater range of experiences between different listeners. Hence the relation of sound art to the plastic arts – listeners 'assemble' the work from different perspectives, directions, and timescales. But this is clearly too simple a distinction to make between sound art and music. Perhaps the listener can wander aimlessly through a narrative 'musical' work and also create real dramatic form from a sound installation. The clue to bringing together these two approaches may lie with the nature of the ritual and its participants.

This provocation develops ideas first suggested in 'New spaces/new places: a Sound House for the performance of electroacoustic music and sonic art', *Organised Sound* 6(2) (2001) pp. 103–105.

Thomas Gardner

The interaction between musicians has been one of the traditional strengths of music: it includes an audience and ritual participants but has its origins in group activity, the interpersonal responses of one musician to another.

Sound art, on the other hand, gives validity to types of hearing that do not originate in deliberate collective action, for example in soundscape or acousmatic listening.

Neither of these positions is absolute, and both always include elements of the other. I wish to explore a possibly fictional link between them, which turns on the symmetries and correspondences between two specially coined terms: reciprocal mimesis and grounded mimesis, with reciprocal mimesis linked to notions of mutual entrainment (people singing or playing together), and grounded mimesis to the representation of the audio environment and sound objects within that environment. In current debates that seek to develop the relations between sound art and music, an examination of the notional category difference between these types of mimesis may be helpful. In this light, it can be remarked that the words 'activity' and 'listening' stand at the threshold between the two concepts: in grounded mimesis it is the individual act of listening that is in the foreground, whilst in reciprocal mimesis it is mutually engaged action that is to the fore.

First Provocation – Simon Emmerson

Ritual, Sound, and Music

Music/sound example

Jonty Harrison: *Unsound Objects* (opening), crossfades to
Luc Ferrari: *Presque Rien nr.2* (extract), crossfades to
Christina Kubisch: *Oase 2000* (extract)

Mythical origins

Perhaps it is too easy to begin at a mythical beginning – a 'Garden of Eden' view, in which content, listening strategy, and the physical and social environment in which the work was experienced, were once unified and reinforcing and are now rendered increasingly dysfunctional for some kinds of music. A prime example is the opera house with which contemporary music has had a love/hate relationship since 1945.[1] Clearly it will die unless it adapts radically, but there are other less obvious cases. Hearing any music live is different from hearing a recording.[2] If we cannot bring them back into some balanced relationship with their cultural supporting structures then these may follow the opera house into the past.

Categories

I start my provocation with a categorical position, although the idea of such definition is there in order to be criticised, to take apart. How we group things together must always allow flexibility. My initial stance is dualistic[3]: 'music' belongs to an idea of wholeness and completion – the 'beginning-middle-end' paradigm. Ideally each listener has available to him/her the whole experience in broadly the same terms, although of course interpretations may vary considerably. This 'beginning-middle-end' structure is not assumed to be limited solely to a written authored tradition; any performance from a wide range of genres (including jazz, Indian classical music, gamelan, amongst many) can have this characteristic.

Yet this 'music' tradition seems to be described in opposition to much sound art, where the ambulant listener has considerably greater influence (even control) over the experience which might take place asynchronously, at different times for each participant. Perhaps the work draws the listener in, captures the imagination and encourages an extended visit – or perhaps not. The variety of experiences is potentially much greater in an installative sound art work than in (say) concert music.

This contrast of approaches seems to be indicative of whether the artist intends a sense of wholeness and completeness of the experience a priori or whether that finally rests within the listener's control to define. It further contrasts 'formed works' against 'open experiences'[4] as we have noted, but clearly ignores the vital contribution from popular musicologies, which forcefully argues with the dominance of 'work' in our discourse. The approach of these newer musicologies stresses much more the processes by which music (for example a 'jazz song' standard) is interpreted, shared, transformed, and transmitted without the notion of a single ideal 'work'. Do these newer musicologies rely on an equivalent sense of a priori wholeness? This is much less clear and will depend on genre and performance circumstance. In many cases the 'beginning-middle-end' paradigm will still apply: even in music that is not strictly notated there may still be a strong expectation by the listener as to how the music is structured.

Plots

Parallels have often been drawn between the 'plots' and 'storytelling' of literature[5] and the narrative forms of much of the world's music. I would hazard a risky generalisation that the term 'composer' tends to relate to a tradition of written plot construction and development. Counter to this, many of my students would describe themselves as musicians or artists. They do not recognise themselves as 'composers' at all, preferring a term with (as they see it) less historical baggage and less reliance on written 'scores'. Yet they, too, often construct narrative musical forms much as oral storytellers. Now all of these groups (whatever they call themselves) are the authors of the plot, but in relation to some sound art the 'authorial voice' has shifted towards the *listener* – or at least we can say there is some shared responsibility between the composer and the listener for the sounding 'storyline'.

So the counterbalance against the beginning-middle-end paradigm involves the listeners, and their active participation in the forming of their individual experiences of the work. I use the term forming deliberately in contrast to 'form' because it cannot exist a priori – it is created on the fly. Whereas the potential of a 'fully formed' work – at least to some degree – does exist beforehand. Hence there are two contrasting approaches: the one is about the totality of the work; the other about many simultaneous possibly asynchronous experiences which nonetheless touch and interweave. So the task for both the practitioner and the theorist is to come to terms with these different ways of telling stories.

The two, form and forming, are not entirely the same: we can dip into and out of a formed work, too, of course, but there is much greater constraint on the alternatives. We do not have earlids to close and so, sitting in a fixed seat, we tend to stay put and remain to a degree subject to the ongoing sound. There is also the cultural ideal and maybe expectation that we should at least try to get a sense of the whole as conceived by the composer. I do however acknowledge that clear distinctions tend to break down in certain musical traditions – even of so-called 'concert music' – that undermines the teleological principle of much Western art upon which the traditional 'beginning-middle-end' paradigm (and Booker's narratives) is based: minimalism, for example, or many of the works of Morton Feldman. Stockhausen in discussing his 'moment form'[6] ideas distinguished processes that 'start' and 'stop' rather than 'begin' and 'end' (Stockhausen 1963, p. 207; Wörner 1973 pp. 109–10). His distinction of those terms is a reminder of the 'tuning in and out' metaphor he used elsewhere; the radio is always 'receiving the total flux' – we choose to switch on, tune, listen and switch off. The receiver's experience is not defined by the sender. Soap opera offers an interesting comparison in this context: at one level it is a 'flux' – 'life goes on... and on...' We can dip in and out of it often with a considerable gap: we may have been away for a year but can catch up quite quickly. But at another level soaps weave the basic plots more locally and shorter term: characters enact their journeys from rags to riches, quests, comedies, and tragedies in small interconnecting scenes.

Such scenarios pose a challenge. There is always some movement within continuity, but how are the shapes within that flux generated?[7] Might the sound artist want to create a sense of narrative, a sense of direction, a sense of the non-arbitrariness at the short timescale but continuity within the long-term – something more than just picking up an amuse-bouche (amuse-oreille?). How to get the newly engaged listener to participate, to become involved; how to build into that involvement a sense of surprise, even shock (the sudden movement of a Tinguely sculpture, for example) that might generate a dramatic (moment) form, which may or may not demand some kind of resolution. If we have indeed lost the plot I am challenging the sound artist to make starting and stopping into beginning and ending, and would like to ask how this might be made into a significant activity in negotiation with the listener/participant.

Ritual renewal

I suggest we need to consider again the notion of ritual. A ritual reaffirms something, often, though not always, collectively. Christopher Small took musicking[8] (including that found in the traditional Western musical concert) to be such a ritual, which affirmed the collective values of the group, its continuity and identity.[9] Whether this ritual strictly needs a narrative or not is debateable. However, we need to develop rituals in music and the sound arts which are more inclusive – and thus are unlike the alienation inherent in the rituals of many modern musical forms, which appear to have become the preserve of a specialised group. To do this we must re-engage with ritual that is more under control of the user – who both belongs to and needs the artwork to add meaning and value to life in some way. It may not be necessary to embrace the wholesale populism of soap opera, but its idea of weaving smaller scale dramatic 'stories' into the ongoing flux is a possible strategy we might develop.

A substantial part of the ritual is the social construction of the experience which will influence how I listen to the sound material of the artwork. Where is the listening taking place? Who am I with? Listening in an opera house is quite different from that in a venue 'under the arches'. All music and sound art is site-specific; while sometimes built for specific physical spaces, the idea of site or place includes the social dimension of the performance, the way listeners move and interact within the area of the artwork. In addition, the sound material itself makes demands on the listener. In an installation the sound might demand attention and focused listening and the final forming of the work thus becomes a real-time negotiation between environment, sound material, and listener – with specific issues of timing, both institutional and personal. I have already argued that this creates the possibility for a wide range of 'plots',[10] and that the task for the artist is to engage with these options. To what extent are the possibilities of the work circumscribed, to what extent entirely open and visitor-created? It might be possible at last to create a kind of common ground between the 'beginning-middle-end' tradition and the sound installation open form.

All the three sound examples I presented at the beginning of this provocation are normally experienced in different settings that seem to demand different listening approaches. Interestingly, however, their materials overlap: the Jonty Harrison plays on 'natural sounds and extended acousmatic listening', the Luc Ferrari engages an embodied soundscape (with the author/composer present) with a strong expressionist undertone, while the Christina Kubisch demands (at least in the original) the listener's active intervention in creating the soundscape in the first place. I am trying to keep them apart not push them together into a single listening mode: each has its own particular ideal performance ritual. In the final part of the music/sound example I presented we heard Kubisch's *Oase 2000,* from the Sonic Boom exhibition at the Hayward Gallery in the year 2000. In the original you made a mix for yourself as you walked through the installation area interacting directly with the induction loops – but what you heard here was from the CD. It is one person's version, one 'walk through'.[11]

Minority interest and renewal

I argue that it is necessary to make a distinction between an elite (when it becomes a privileged group)[12] and a minority interest. Classical music seems clearly to have claimed elite status. It has in the past demanded a kind of exclusivity with respect to (even superiority over) other musical forms.[13] While much disputed within anthropology, ethnomusicology, and popular-music studies – and in recent years within the classical community itself – the essence of this claim remains alive within many dominant teaching and research institutions and conservatoires of music. Let us instead try to imagine a model without this elite status. A way forward might be to create a more ecological system around a network of minority interests. Minorities must be preserved; minorities are the stuff of reinvention. There are parallels with issues of biodiversity: we need a variety of seed-corn types to help protect against unknowable future changes in the environment or diseases, or we risk catastrophe. A diverse culture of minority interests has richer possibilities for innovation, interaction, adaptation to change, and the generation of the unexpected.

Conclusion

The very creation of a continuum (in effect an open field rather than a line) from 'formed' (music) to 'open' (sound art) is part of the inexorable shift away from grand (central) narratives and Eurocentric definitions. But I suspect that it is the 'grand' (and central) part of the phrase that has been discredited. A narrative aspect may be encountered in many cultures and will not lightly disappear. Without its historical baggage the beginning-middle-end paradigm may well survive in a varied and healthy form, but it might be more liable to interact with other possible forming strategies.

This is where we bring two themes together. If the rituals of Western art music (whether so-called mainstream or avant-garde) are part of a 'top-down' tradition that is – whatever its definition – elitist, the question becomes what kinds of more open rituals might emerge. The ritual and the artistic forming processes are completely symbiotic – one interlocks with the other.[14] Attend a traditional concert and – at least until recently – you would be present for the beginning, the middle, and the end. If the authority for formation of the ritual is now more delegated, or is at least a negotiation between artist/producer and listener/viewer, all within a social context, then our open field becomes much more creative and potentially inclusive.

In 2001, at the 'Music without Walls' conference at De Montfort University (organised by Leigh Landy), I described three contrasted listening spaces: 'Club space: sampled focus listening: open works – Quiet space: extensive focus listening: formed works – Installation space: sampled and extensive focus listening: formed and open works.'

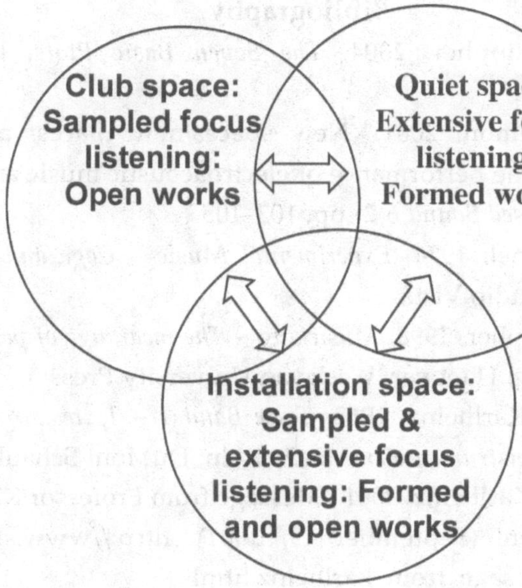

I believe these three spaces are now increasingly blurring at the edges and overlapping. There is much greater potential for interaction between them, although at their heart the differences in listening strategies are still apparent. I believed then that the most problematic space was the 'quiet space' that demanded extensive and focused listening. This generally means both the exclusion of external sound and the minimising of internally generated sound, including that created through social interaction. Once again this is too simply seen as a historical product of the Western 'classical' tradition. Of course there are many traditions of music that demand detailed and focused listening.[15] We need to rethink the sociality of such spaces – for example, the role of a 'forward' direction or a proscenium; how we might create the more relaxed and friendly surroundings now commonly demanded. I still believe we should build sound houses, rather like public-access versions of the Bauhaus, where music and sound art may coexist, interact, and generate new forms.

Bibliography

Booker, Christopher. 2004. *The Seven Basic Plots*. London: Continuum.

Emmerson, Simon. 2001. 'New spaces/new places: a Sound House for the performance of electroacoustic music and sonic art.' *Organised Sound* 6(2) pp. 103–105.

Nyman, Michael. 1974. *Experimental Music – Cage and Beyond*. London: Studio Vista.

Small, Christopher. 1998. *Musicking – The meanings of performing and listening*. Hanover: Wesleyan University Press.

Stockhausen, Karlheinz. 1963. *Texte Band 1 – Texte zur elektronischen und instrumentalen Musik*. Köln: DuMont Schauberg.

Stockhausen, Karlheinz. 2001. 'Message from Professor Karlheinz Stockhausen' (September 19, 2001). http://www.stockhausen.org/message_from_karlheinz.html

Toop, David. 1995. *Ocean of Sound: aether talk, ambient sound and imaginary worlds*. London: Serpent's Tail.

Wörner, Karl. 1973. *Stockhausen, life and work*. London: Faber and Faber.

Introductory sound/music examples

Ferrari, Luc. 1995. *Presque Rien nr.2* on: *Presque Rien*, CD, INA/GRM-MUSIDISC: 254172.

Harrison, Jonty. 1996. *Unsound Objects* on: *Articles indéfinis*, CD, Empreintes Digitales: IMED 9627.

Kubisch, Christina. 2000. *Oase 2000* on: CD with book *Sonic Boom* (exhibition catalogue), London: Hayward Gallery.

Notes

1 For example Pierre Boulez, who was in favour of 'burning down opera houses' until he chose to be conductor for the centenary Bayreuth Festival in 1976; or Philip Glass, who moved from being a member of the New York downtown art scene to that of the Metropolitan Opera and international

circuit.

2 The colloquium included discussions of the relationship between notated traditions and more open ones, as well as the role of recording in the transmission of performance practice.

3 During the colloquium, in a response to Volkmar Klien's provocation, Cathy Lane cited Salomé Voegelin's abstract and developed the idea that these are not two opposing poles but points on a continuum of possibilities between 'music' and 'sound art' – I shall discuss this further below.

4 'Formed works' are largely defined (probably written down) by the composer, whereas 'open works' leave aspects free for the performer (or the listener) to choose or develop.

5 These parallels are brilliantly analysed in Christopher Booker's *The Seven Basic Plots: Why we tell stories* (2004); although this book is highly critical of 'the modern turn' in plot construction.

6 Stockhausen also described this 'moment form' as 'unending form' (Wörner 1973, p. 108).

7 I include generation through chance procedures (Cage and beyond) as an option for such flux generation.

8 Christopher Small proposed this definition of musicking: 'To music is to take part, in any capacity, in a musical performance, whether by performing, by listening, by rehearsing or practicing, by providing material for performance (what is called composing), or by dancing' (1998, p. 9).

9 Strictly, Small called this a 'ceremony' at which 'the values – which is to say, the concepts of what constitute right relationships – of that group are explored, affirmed and celebrated' (1998, p. 183).

10 Booker's list of the seven basic plots: Overcoming the Monster, Rags to Riches, The Quest, Voyage and Return, Comedy, Tragedy, Rebirth, Precursors.

11 David Toop explained at the colloquium that there were copyright problems associated with this installation as the

environmental recordings had not been made by the artist.

12 At the colloquium other contributors defended the idea of 'elite' (especially when 'anyone could join'), which I accept except when – as is the case cited here – the group concerned claims privileged treatment by society at large. I think there are two definitions of elite at work here.

13 Successive avant-gardes within Western classical music have believed themselves to be 'heirs of Beethoven', out ahead of the mainstream yet renewers of that same grand tradition. Clearly the term 'avant-garde' is now used more generally with respect to innovative practices than when Michael Nyman made this clear characterisation as distinct from 'experimental' music (Nyman 1974).

14 This is essentially Christopher Small's point, but this view stands against a more 'transcendental' (Platonic) view of the artwork, which still determines much (Western) musical discourse.

15 Such detailed and focused listening is what Pauline Oliveros for example has encapsulated in her 'deep listening' enterprise (see www.deeplistening.org). And there are many other examples from a wide range of genres (Toop 1995).

Second Provocation – Thomas Gardner
Reciprocal Mimesis and Grounded Mimesis

The interaction between musicians has been one of the traditional strengths of music: it includes an audience and ritual participants but has its origins in group activity, the interpersonal responses of one musician to another.

Sound art, on the other hand, gives validity to types of hearing that do not originate in deliberate collective action, for example in soundscape or acousmatic listening.

Neither of these positions is absolute, and in this provocation I wish to explore a series of links between them, which turn on the symmetries and correspondences between two specially coined terms: reciprocal mimesis and grounded mimesis, where reciprocal mimesis is linked to notions of mutual entrainment (people singing or playing together), and grounded mimesis to the representation of the non-musical audio environment and sound objects within that environment.

These two terms are not proposed in order to establish fixed entities, but are intended to function as temporary placeholders, allowing for the development of a range of interrelated ideas, which will be briefly elaborated on.

Firstly, to define the two terms a little more clearly. Reciprocal mimesis can be understood as an extension of 'entrainment', which is a significant element in negotiating the sonic relationship between musicians and is discussed by researchers from a variety of backgrounds, for example ethnomusicology and biomusicology (Wallin 1991; Cross 2007; Mithen 2006; Dissanayake 2001). Entrainment can be described as the way in which two or more people attune to each other using mimetic patterns of behaviour, simultaneously reflecting and internalising the other in a reciprocal construct.

The feature that distinguishes reciprocal mimesis from grounded mimesis is that the reciprocation actually produces change in the person who is the subject of mimesis – indeed; participants are simultaneously subject and object in this kind of mimetic feedback system. Daniel Stern's analysis of mother–infant relations (Stern 1977) shows one way in which this area of mimesis can be approached, observing the co-production and regulation of vitality effects and their contribution to the development of an infant's identity. Other fields of research offer other analytic approaches, for example evolutionary musicology and group improvisation all take the reciprocal interaction between people as a key feature. It is to be noted that this direction of research is in distinction to more orthodox music analysis, which has a greater focus on those aspects of musical structure that are 'internal' to the music, for example, in systems for organising pitch and rhythm.

By comparison the term 'grounded mimesis' focuses on the relationship between listener and sonic environment, and not on the interaction between the musicians themselves. The characteristic that distinguishes this kind of mimesis from reciprocal mimesis is that the environment or object represented is not itself materially changed by the process of representation. For example, listening to Hildegard Westerkamp's Kits Beach Soundwalk (1989) or Luc Ferrari's *Presque Rien no.1 ou le lever du jour au bord de la mer* (1970) does not produce a reciprocal change in the beach, coastline, or village recorded.

As another example, when an improvising group uses electronic sounds generated outside the circle of the musicians, for example location recordings, the process of inclusion of these 'other' sounds into musical practice results in change for the musicians and the musical culture, but not for the object represented. Much sound art makes use of these kinds of grounded mimesis, where the sources of the recorded or synthesised sounds are not present and thus are not able to listen back. As with the reciprocal mimesis discussed above, grounded mimesis too is marginalised in more traditional forms of musicology where it is usually positioned in the subcategory of program music.[1]

However, the point of this provocation is not to fix a fundamental difference in the substance of these types of mimesis, but to explore some of the ways in which this binary is opened out or deconstructed. I will offer two very different examples of ways in which the relationship between grounded and reciprocal mimesis can be interpreted, one of which veers towards the schizophrenic, the other towards a more idealistic fusion. The schizophrenic version explores the disruptive effects of media technology on instruments and group music-making, whilst the more idealistic version focuses on the connection between dancing and the sound walk.

Schizophrenic conception

Jean-Luc Nancy uses the example of a face to illustrate the way in which individual exposure plays an explicit part in being together:

> "my" face always exposed to others, always turned toward an other and faced by him or her, never facing myself. This is the archi-original impossibility of Narcissus that opens straight away onto the possibility of the political. (Nancy 1991, p. xxxviii)

In terms of the sound-making of a group, the performer's voice or instrument provides the acoustic face which may be turned to an other, and through which an individual may become present in the politics of being together. The audibility of a performer's gestures, and the link between the gesture and sound, is the starting point from which reciprocal mimesis in sound-making can occur.

However, the 'faceless' (in terms of an individual gendered performer) electronic voice of a synthesised sound or recorded soundscape allows grounded mimesis to enter into sonic culture. By playing a recording, switching on a radio, or monitoring an internet site one can be in the presence of sound sources which are not listening back and which are not participating in the here-and-now interchanges of the group. This creates a significant space for new conceptions of the instrument, mediating between the reciprocal voice of the musician and the voice of a technologically mediated other. This new kind of instrument may act as a bridge between grounded and reciprocal mimesis, moving between the musician's individual voice and new forms of technologised presence.

To elaborate on some of the implications of this I give the following example: I have been working on a particular conception of the electronic instrument, called the Ouija board, which is used by two performers who work in a group alongside other acoustic musicians.[2] The shadow of the Ouija players' hands acts as a control mechanism. Thus, the gaze of the performer is not only on their hands as they appear before them, connected to their body, but also looks at the shadow that the hands cast on the instrument surface, which controls the production of sound (using a camera that analyses the depth and dimensions of the shadow). The shadow acts as a metaphor as well as literal controller since, along with its visual representation of the hand as a shadow, it enables a different relationship with electronically mediated sound. Rather than thinking of the loudspeakers as simply another form of presence, to be treated in a similar way to the sound-making of a live musician, the sound is experienced, like the shadow of the hand, as a negative imprint left by the sounding object. The performer of the 'Ouija' becomes engaged in a form of mediumship, listening out for and finding new places for these ghosts of sound sources.

The expanded context of this 'negative imprint' can be further clarified by considering its relation to Sigmund Freud's conception of the shadow in his essay on 'Mourning and Melancholia'. Describing a patient suffering from melancholia he wrote: 'The shadow of the object fell upon the ego, and the latter could henceforth be judged by a special agency, as though it were an object, the forsaken object' (Freud 1957, p. 256).

Recorded sound can perpetuate the traces of the lost object, simulating, in a mechanical way, the shadow objects created by the sufferer of melancholia or schizophrenia. This new kind of sound is in a fine balance between melancholia and the preservation of corpses: 'radio bodies are nobodies' (Whitehead 1991, p. 85). As Allen S. Weiss details in his book *Breathless* (2002), the technical prosthesis provided by recorded sound is a potent instrument in the shift from 19th-century lyrical nostalgia to the schizophrenic, multi-centred sensibility of postmodern identity.

This schizophrenic critique of musical togetherness introduced via the extended mourning of mediatised sound production exemplifies one of the ways in which reciprocal mimesis and grounded mimesis encounter each other. It emphasises the place of media technology and the role mediatised sound plays in new forms of group music-making and instrument design.

This schizophrenic example will now be followed by a more idealistic one, which places less emphasis on the significance of mediatisation as a link between reciprocal and grounded mimesis, and instead focuses on the way in which they allow a connection to be made between dancing a minuet and walking in the city.

Idealistic conception

The dérive is an experimental form of walking (Debord 1981; Solnit 2001) which holds an emblematic position in the listening experience of contemporary sound art, allowing the extended act of moving through urban space to thread together diverse and potentially discordant listening experiences. The walker in this scenario is exploring a particular kind of grounded mimesis, allowing themselves to be changed by the atmospheres and geography that they encounter during the walk. The object of the walk does not lie in a particular destination, but in an appreciation of chance encounters, emphasising the liberty of movement unimpeded by barricades, defying ghettos or social containment.

The minuet can be said to hold a similar though reversed position in relation to music of the early 18th century, in which the musical structure of the minuet allows the constrained space of the dance floor to become the site for extended explorations of social engagement, regulated through the flow and breaking of the minuet's musical time. Whilst free improvisation allows for the emergence of new kinds of reciprocal mimesis, the formalisation of structures in the minuet allows a greater integration with existing social practices, and thus a wider potential for participation and engagement. The staging of contact between genders, the nature of the participation of onlookers, and the manifestation of other socially sanctioned expressions of equality and hierarchy are brought into a particular performative realisation by the musical structure of the minuet. These do not represent every possible encounter, but allow particular, and socially valued, models of reciprocity to be enacted and explored.

The difference between minuet and dérive can be seen as a question of displacement, and how displacement is realised, contained, or released within the conception of the work. The third beat of the minuet, for example, does not align with the biped gait of human walking and is symptomatic of further asymmetries of beat, harmony, and choreography that permeate the structure (Russell 1992; Pierce 2008). The dérive may be seen as sound art's inversion or fulfilment of the process of displacement, in that its ideal form is carried out with no destination in mind – thus the gap or displacement is no longer 'within' the work but is a suspended pause around it, with a destination unresolved but consisting of various potential stopping points.

That these two practices, minuet and dérive, might seem so disconnected from each other is more a problem of conception than something innate. The difference between dancing and walking is not in fact so great, as John Cage's 1977 composition *49 Waltzes for the Five Boroughs* already suggests.

Conclusion: walking and sauntering

A successful volte-face between reciprocal mimesis and grounded mimesis depends on our ability to walk creatively. Our awareness of the shadowy origins of the sonic object requires that we leave the destination of this walk open or sans-terre ('without-ground'), so we might, to paraphrase Henry Thoreau, saunter to Elysium. This might be an optimistic hope, but the impetus behind this provocation is the belief that by considering reciprocal mimesis and grounded mimesis together one becomes aware not only of exclusionary differences between musical and sound art practice, and also of ways in which a richer relationship can be conceived: Perhaps in some sense landscapes do have ears and can listen back?

Bibliography

Cage, John. 1977. *49 Waltzes for the Five Boroughs: for performer(s) or listener(s) or record maker(s)*. Vol. 66735. Henmar Press.

Cross, Ian. 2007. 'The evolutionary nature of musical meaning.' *Musicae Scientiae*.

Cusack, Peter. 2012. *Sounds from dangerous places*. ReR Megacorp.

Debord, Guy, and Ken Knabb. 1981. 'Situationist International Anthology.' Berkeley: Bureau of Public Secrets.

Dissanayake, Ellen. 2001. 'An Ethological View of Music and its Relevance to Music Therapy.' *Nordic Journal of Music Therapy*, 10 (2). pp. 159–175.

Ferrari, Luc. 1995. *Presque Rien no.1 ou le lever du jour au bord de la mer*. Ina-GRM (INA C2008).

Freud, Sigmund. 1957. 'Mourning and melancholia.' *Standard Edition*, 14. pp. 237–58. London: Hogarth Press.

Mithen, Steven J. 2006. *The Singing Neanderthals: The origins of music, language, mind, and body*. Cambridge: Harvard University Press.

Nancy, Jean-Luc. 1991. *The Inoperative Community*. University of Minnesota Press.

Pierce, Ken. 2008. 'Choreographic Structure in Baroque Dance.' *Dance, Spectacle, and the Body Politick, 1250-1750*, 182.

Russell, Tilden A. 1992. 'The unconventional dance minuet: Choreographies of the Menuet d'Exaudet.' *Acta Musicologica*, 64(2), pp. 118–138.

Solnit, Rebecca. 2001. *Wanderlust: A history of walking*. Penguin Group USA.

Stern, Daniel. 1977. *The First Relationship: Infant and Mother*. Cambridge: Harvard University Press.

Thoreau, Henry D. 2006. *Walking*. Cosimo, Inc. Retrieved from http://books.google.co.uk/books?hl=en&lr=&id=rVZQfYsxw3sC&oi=fnd&pg=PT5&dq=thoreau+walking&ots=dQsE7nKQQy&sig=SravoVsMRARO7mdjQ_8plYTJ6cs

Wallin, Nils L. 1991. *Biomusicology: Neurophysiological, neuropsychological, and evolutionary perspectives on the origins and purposes of music* (Vol. 68). Pendragon Press.

Westerkamp, Hildegard. 1996. *Kits Beach Soundwalk* (1989). *On Transformations*. Empreintes Digitales, IMED, 9631.

Weiss, Allen S. 2002. *Breathless: sound recording, disembodiment, and the transformation of lyrical nostalgia*. Wesleyan University Press.

Whitehead, Gregory. 1991. 'Holes in the Head: A Theatre for Radio Operations.' *Performing Arts Journal*, 13(3), pp. 85–91.

Notes

1 Program music is the name given to music that carries an explicitly 'extramusical' meaning, for example Beethoven's *Pastoral Symphony* or Berlioz's *Symphonie Fantastique*.

2 The group is called the Automatic Writing Circle (http://automaticwritingcircle.org.uk). They are from diverse musical backgrounds, amongst them: historically informed performance, noise musics, electroacoustic composition, experimental, and popular music. The Ouija board itself consists of a white sheet, a light, and a camera linked to software which analyses the depth and dimensions of shadows.

Transcript of Third Colloquium Discussion

David Toop: Simon, interesting point about Christina Kubisch. She got the Hayward Gallery in big trouble, because she took that recording from a British Library recording without acknowledging it. The recordist heard the piece and recognised it and was incensed. Her reaction was very high-handed, she said: 'I don't care, it does not matter.' The Hayward Gallery had to clear up the mess. But it is of interest because we have been talking about territories all morning, and differences of strategy in terms of the way in which material is approached. Her strategy was just to say 'I like this this, it's mine', and his strategy was to say 'This is not art, it's documentation, and it's not yours'.

There was another point, you were talking about listening from beginning to end, and you included Javanese gamelan. I recently had occasion to re-read Colin McPhee's book *House in Bali*, which is not terribly reliable, because he missed out his wife for example, and he also missed out his interest in young Balinese boys. But he talks about one of these all-night rituals, and there are many occasions during those rituals where people, including the performers, fall asleep and have to be woken up. You are absolutely right, there is a beginning and end, there is a trajectory, which must be followed. But the way you honour that trajectory is very different, and that is one of our problems, isn't it. We seem to have ended up with a very limited number of options of how we honour a particular trajectory, so it becomes harder and harder for us to actually engage with anything fully. Because, you are either on or off.

Simon Emmerson: I think that is profoundly true, just as you can dip in and out of a soap opera even though it has an enormously long trajectory. You catch up very quickly in a structure like that, partly because of things we were talking about before lunch; and because there is a tradition of it and you have an expectation.

Nye Parry: I wrote that soap-opera analogy down when you said it. You were talking very much about trajectories and things ending, but soap operas don't, and that is actually part of the attraction: that they don't end, and in that way they reflect real life much more. So you do dip in and out, and I think you also probably dip in and out of individual stories; to that extent they are open form. There might be a character that you have no interest in whatsoever and you might go and make a cup of tea every time that character is on the screen, and you might end up drinking a lot of tea. In terms of the guy sitting in that room up there, I don't think it is the open form that is a problem, because that is something that is engaged with within the form of the soap opera.

Allen S. Weiss: It's interesting because in the 1960s, in cinema, music, and a number of the arts, experimentation was beginning with extremely long forms, long in relation to what was considered the standard length of the genre. For some of these long durations transformed spectatorship. One thinks for example of Andy Warhol's quip about the way to see *Empire*; he said, 'Well you come in, you see some of the film, you go out and have dinner, you wait in the hall, you talk to some friends, and you go back you see a little more'. He was half joking, but the other half really spoke to new transformations of how we can deal with pieces which are sometimes beyond the limits of the genres we are used to and sometimes physically beyond the possibilities of listening straight through from beginning to end.

Robert Worby: But doesn't that happen with any piece of music? I am sure most of us only actually listen for about thirty seconds before we drift off and come back and drift off and come back and drift off. I went to hear Morton Feldman's *For John Cage*, which is eighty minutes. It felt like twenty minutes, but I was aware that I wasn't listening to every single chord that was played, and it's the same with any Mahler symphony, or a three-minute pop song. I can't listen to a three-minute pop song all the way through.

Stephen Preston: Isn't that part of listening, the attention and focus is constantly shifting, the way we drift is very much part of listening. I can see what you are getting at with this idea of a totality and its construction, but surely all listening is always a construction, it is a question of enculturation more than of the music itself.

Simon: Yes that's what I mean about a continuum, it is clearly always constructed by the listener. But nonetheless, even if we don't listen to every bar of a Mahler symphony it is there as a total thing.

Claudia Molitor: Are you talking about the intention of the person who has made the work? So the intention of the composer is one of a listening that the composer has constructed for the listener, whereas the intention of the sound artist might be to say, well I am giving listening opportunities to the audience.

Simon: Oh clearly, because in fact I think what you have just said, and what Allen has just said, those are the examples of works that do not have strong forms. In other words, well-formedness is really what I am referring to, and of course we construct that. Clearly a LaMonte Young or a Feldman are going to be listened to in a different way, they are challenging you to listen in a different way.

Robert: Oh absolutely. I do not think that is a narrative though.

Salomé Voegelin: But I think there is something else to that totality. If I can come from the other side, from a sound art side. I think that some of the problems of a listener not listening to a totality, however unformed or ephemeral this totality might be, is the context of the gallery and the expectations it sets up. If I go to a gallery I can pop in and out, I can have a quick look at the sculpture, a quick look at the painting, a quick listen, and I am out again, when actually that is part of the problem for me with sound art in a gallery – it's that impatience, the not-lingering, when some works require a lingering listening.

Nye: And video suffers the same way that sound art does.

Salomé: Absolutely.

Robert: But doesn't painting and sculpture too. Wasn't there some work done in the National Gallery looking at the audiences looking at paintings and most people look at painting for three seconds and then they move to the next one.

Thomas Gardner: I just want to come back to your idea of listening for forty seconds and then zoning out. Perhaps zoning out is part of listening? That the way in which they link to each other can develop while you are listening, they can become integrated in a different way as the piece evolves, as your experience of yourself going in and out of the piece evolves. And this is something that seems right. It seems pejorative to say 'I have zoned out', when possibly you can never completely really zone in.

Robert: I think it is to do with detail. Listening to the Feldman, the Feldman is made up of loops, and there are four beats and five beats, and listening really intensely one is aware that there are five beats in that repetition and there are four beats in this one and three and a half beats in that one, and when you have not been listening for ten seconds you have not got the detail, you've lost the detail of what is happening in the pattern.

Justin Yang: Would it be worth mentioning Bergson and qualitative time here? I like to try to think about the musical experience in a qualitative sense. So when you were saying Feldman in twenty minutes: Feldman talks extensively about scale, and pieces over an hour inhabit a different realm of the human psychology than twenty-minute ones, so I think it is worth thinking about qualitative time too. In a Bergsonian sense, is that forty seconds looking at the artwork a lifetime, or a significantly, qualitatively, temporally significant experience?

Aura Satz: Can I ask Simon, just in relation to that, are you suggesting that the art form itself dictates the kind of attention it receives?

Simon: I am issuing this as a challenge. I must stress that the whole point of setting up these two opposites is exactly about finding the common ground. Already I have been very affected by two remarks; one is that we construct a narrative piece by sampling, which is profoundly true. I have said the wrong thing to Claudia a minute ago, I said 'that is not a narrative', and of course it is, it is the multiple storytelling these days, rather than the single storyteller, and that's quite clearly a common ground: multiple plots.

Sorry could you repeat your question again, I am losing the plot myself [laughter].

Aura: My question was whether the music, or the material form of the sound, dictates its own mode of listening. Whether there's a kind of material construct that dictates, that prescribes how it gets listened to?

Simon: Yes, plus the third thing I mentioned this morning: the environment. So in other words, the social construction will influence how I listen to the material of the composition. Where is it? If it is in an opera house or somewhere I will listen to it in a different way even if it is identical sonically, so all music is to a degree site-specific, all, the whole lot. 18th-century, 19th-century, 20th-century, it was composed for certain specific spaces and that influences the way you listen to it. So I say yes, the material does make a demand on listening practice, but so does the environment you are in and the people you meet.

Robert: I was taken by something Salomé and Steven said this morning, when they were talking about listening. They said 'I put on Brahms', you said, meaning a CD, but I thought of it as a cloak. So what you are doing is putting on a CD but you are putting on a cloak, and I wonder whether when you are listening to the CD you are doing the washing up, or looking after your kids, or you are doing something else, whereas in the concert hall listening to Brahms you are not putting on Brahms at all, you are going to Brahms.

Salomé: Yes, unfortunately I have very rarely the leisure where I can just say I am going to do ninety minutes of Brahms pure. So yes there will probably be kids in the other room, and there will be things to be done. Also, due to the same circumstances I very rarely go to Brahms. But I quite like that. In the same way that I quite liked how, in the piece you played Simon, I thought I heard a rubbish truck, you know the vehicle-reversing sound, beepbeepbeepbeep, was that in your piece? Because that was a nice moment, of something being part of the soundscape and being part of the composition, and I thought that fitted in nicely, but it sounded like a rubbish truck reversing.

Simon: I think that is an amazing observation because it's actually an animal I believe. He was out in the desert somewhere recording something and lo and behold these animals sound like rubbish trucks.

Salomé: Maybe it is because I work here and there are a lot of rubbish trucks reversing, so again it is about context. Thus to go back to you Rob, I am actually very happy that Brahms mingles with kids, and with my life, and then it is my Brahms and it is my contingent participation and interpretation, and for me that is maybe the only way to listen.

Robert: I had another observation, when Simon talked about sound art you said 'on and off', and that made me think of digital 1 and 0s, in a banal kind of way. It occurred to me that sound art, as we are talking about it, has been around for ten or twenty years in the form that we are talking about. And maybe that is to do with the fact that it is easy now to record sound, everybody has a digital recorder and they can record sound very, very easily. Whereas prior to that time it was extremely difficult to record sound. You needed a tape recorder and you needed to plug a microphone into the tape recorder and you needed to plug the tape recorder into something else. And if you wanted to edit you had to cut the tape, and it was very, very difficult to work with the medium of sound so people did not do it very much. And now that we have the digital technology it is extremely easy so it is commonplace. It's kind of everywhere. And this mode of listening that Simon is talking about, 'putting on the sound', is now doable, whereas previously it wasn't doable. I mean there was sound art before, of course there was, but it was not as commonplace as it is now. You can say 'sound art' on the *Today* programme on Radio 4 now, and the audience sort of knows what you are talking about.

Claudia: But it relates also to what you were saying Aura, because that technology that facilitates sound art also informs the way we will engage.

Robert: Yes of course it does.

Claudia: And we can say, 'Oh I'll just listen to this for forty seconds', because you know you can go back to it. So, this technology informs the way we listen because we know we do not have to listen to it now. Whereas when we go to a concert, a one-off performance, even if it is of a piece we already know, and we can listen to it again, we know that this instance of the performance is unique, so we might want to linger with it more. Whereas if we pop in to the gallery we know that, unless something horrific happens like a fire, that picture is going to be there next week, and I can look at it again, and accumulate lots of quantitative time. Although I also agree you do not necessarily need a lot of time to get some meaning out of something.

Stephen: It is interesting how we do that now but it was not so in the past of course. I mean you go to the theatre and if somebody like Hamlet did his soliloquy you'd applaud loudly and they would repeat it. A piece of music, like a movement, repeat it, a song, repeat it. In opera don't listen until your favourite singer's on. People would sit on stage and talk to the actors. The actors would only learn the parts that they were speaking and the cue into the part. An interesting reflection on now and then if you like, and our ideas of what constitutes a proper attentional span and a proper focus.

Claudia: Italian opera is still like that. When you go to an Italian opera on the outside they have picnics and nobody will be listening.

Leigh Landy: Simon I did drop my attention, but I paid a lot of attention to your first minute. And I want to go back to that. Because I am just wondering how provocative you were being. In a sense you replied to Cathy's continuum, but in another sense, well you chose the Luc Ferrari piece without its voice, which is the marker of the narrative in an otherwise non-narrative piece. So we get something that in fact according to most definitions has a beginning and does have an end, and thus could qualify as sound art. And now we move on to Christina [Kubisch] who did a kind of Cage-ian installation, and Cage, well he has been embraced by sound art, he has been embraced by all the arts, but we still kind of stick music next to him, and yet Christina, musically trained, does not profile herself within that. And so in relation to the dilemmas that you two [Salomé and Thomas] came up with to bring us all together today, both of those examples are bloody ambiguous.

Simon: They are, that was the entire point. I called it a micro journey. Firstly of course, as David [Toop] knows well, as you walk through the Kubisch piece you do a mix yourself. And of course what you heard is a recording of one person's walk through the gallery for a few minutes. But that was exactly the point, because all of those three pieces use environmental sound, all of them can be played in different environments, and it was precisely that: a formed work that is strongly gestural followed by a maybe arty work followed by a clearly installation work. I wanted to pull them apart in order to push them together, that was the point.

Cathy Lane: I just want to throw something into the discussion. I don't know quite where this is going. In fact, I don't know where the whole conversation is going at the moment, it makes me feel a bit anxious. I want it to go 'somewhere'. And I don't know whether this is going to make it go somewhere, but the whole thing about listening. I mean sure, there is the situation of the gallery you wander in and out of, of the concert hall where you sit in the lovely comfortable seat, but what no one has mentioned is money, the economics of the situation – in the gallery invariably you don't pay, at least you do not pay per piece. You haven't parted with money, often you just go in and out. Whereas in the concert you have parted with £20, and you will damn well sit there even if you are going to have a snooze. I don't think we should ignore those issues of how these things are packaged for us. The idea that we have a free will, that we approach these things as total free agents, is actually nonsensical.

Robert: So it comes back to this idea of expectation that was raised earlier today, which I think is linked to tradition: the tradition that sound art comes from is not the same that music comes from, they do overlap obviously. I keep thinking that Cage, and Cage keeps coming up. I do not think that it was a coincidence that he was a friend of Marcel Duchamp.

David: I was asked questions by a broadsheet journalist in an interview recently. The question that stuck out most for me was: 'Is it right that there should be music that doesn't make money in our society?' It took me a while to frame a suitable response. This goes back to Simon's point about making rituals. How can you do that when people have the idea that any music that does not make money is not legitimate in our society, and of course that is a question about what kind of society we have, or we are thinking about at the moment, and music is just a part of it. How can we make new structures?

Seth Ayyez: I was thinking about you mentioning Freud, and the shadow of the object falls across the ego. I just wonder whether there is something in this conversation about mourning the loss of music. Loss of music as something which is, I am not talking about absolute music, but I am talking about music that has intrinsic use-value on its own terms as opposed to as a commodified and monetised exchange token, and the corresponding historic shift from the certain status that music in its capital M no longer has. Are we mourning? This whole question about the distinction between art and music, I am wondering whether below this is a melancholia, a kind of mourning.

John Drever: It is also about the death of the composer with a capital C I think. I have been teaching for some time now but I cannot think of any of my PhD or Masters students that call themselves composers. The C-word is never used, it is such an awkward term to use. There is a reticence, and if you start to call yourself a composer you are like some 19th-century person, from another era, or you are Andrew Lloyd Webber.

Aura: What I am hearing is less the mourning of music but of a mode of attention. We are not lingering enough, and I think that extends beyond the specific medium of sound art or music, it's a more general yearning for a different mode of listening which is a mode of attention, which is what I seem to hear in all of this.

Thomas: It's a way that we can feel that we know why we are here. It is introducing another wonderful possibility that we are presiding either over the murder, death, gradual re-arising of music. I don't know if you put yourself in the murdering place – for a good reason, you know. Does it need to be murdered or is it already dead, and in fact can it die, or does it come back? In this sense Cage is interesting. I think it was because he was not in Europe that he was able to do these thing.

Claudia: You were saying 'does music have to make money', and we instantly think it's a shocking idea, how can we equate art with money? And yes it seems a shocking idea, but isn't it historically a blip that we've had the luxury to make music without having to be connected necessarily to anything else. Because music was always connected to ritual or society, so now it is money rather than ritual, but this idea that it can be just free of everything, that's really maybe a little modernist bubble that is bursting.

Simon: But there are other ways of supporting it. In other words, I think the point about David's remark being so shocking is that it is 'money'. We are not talking about resources, resources is a much broader term. How is a Javanese village gamelan supported? That is a very relevant question. It's a massive orchestra thing in a village. I mean how does it work? The answer is it does, it's in the infrastructure of the social system, and they don't go around counting the coins all the time, it doesn't work that way. What we have to do is to find other means of resource.

Leigh: I have a slightly special spin on this one. Those working in HE at least get these two words thrown at them all the time: 'creative industry'. And it is interesting that the university [De Montfort University] has hired a number of artists who have absolutely nothing to do with nor ever will want to engage with industry. As a student of ethnomusicology, yonks ago, I was taught that in most societies there were three traditions, the third of which has evolved over centuries and is now huge. The first is the music of the people, the music of the community as I would say, the second was a learned music or court music, or art music as we call it here, and finally popular music which I kind of associate with the creative industries. And we have a development taking place currently where all of this is being redefined and the internet not being the least important part in this, as Simon pointed out earlier: folk-community traditions are the most rapidly evolving areas today. The learned music is in association with museum culture and will they continue to exist?

And then you have commercial music. We all accept and hopefully embrace the fact that that ain't going to go away anytime soon. But through the internet there might be further splinterings, and you might get new types of community or tribes forming that will permeate themselves outside the money section.

Now to take that statement and bring it to what we are discussing today, what I have always found fascinating about sound art is that there is already a common ground between those who make it and those who are going to engage with it. Which in experimental contemporary art music was not always the case, it was much more 'I am going to make something that nobody else has made because that will create my identity and my unique selling point'. And 'if nobody understands it that is fine because there is a community that strives on not understanding, and if I don't understand it it is good and I am glad I paid for that'. In sound art, you have all these communities and they are very dynamic, and what fascinates me again, and what I have learned as a trained musician from sound art, is that screaming needs to have common ground.

Salomé: Are you saying that sound artists want common ground?

Leigh: I think that sound art often involves a situation, a context, whether it is a site or a ritual, that people can connect with their lived experience. I have rarely gone to sound art that has no connection with previous experience.

Salomé: I think economics is important, money is important, particularly if you do not only want one sort of sound art and one sort of music that is being sponsored because people are familiar with it in the funding offices. But beside money that we all need and want to live on, for me 'relevance' is a really important term.

Whether it is music or sound art, the stuff with sound has to have a contemporary relevance. I think that is where most of my frustration comes from. I believe that a lot of what is termed 'new classical' music has very little relevance, what is its relevance? And maybe that is the point that music and sound art share, or could share, when they are in the business of sounding now, being relevant and sometimes that doesn't make money, but I think there is another value to it.

Angus Carlyle: Can you explain more what you mean by relevance?

Robert: Yes, I was going to ask that, relevant to what?

Salomé: I think a lot of composition can be very beautiful, it can be entertaining, it can be nice, but it is not necessarily relevant, which is when work engages with its material and what it sounds like now – that's maybe why I am, at least as a provocation, happy to say don't play any dead composers in British concert halls for a year. I would be very interested to see what would happen, what we would fill them with and what we would hear in that year. One of my biggest problems with music, when I go to a conservatoire or a concert, is that is has lost its relevance. It's feeding people who have got the money to sponsor it, who have their opera season-tickets, and to want that, but I don't think it is answering to a contemporary soundscape, it is not listening. I think Brahms – to stay with him – would have listened to his contemporary soundscape, metaphorically and actually, to the sounds around him and what they would have meant. And that would have influenced and informed his compositions.

Simon: Beethoven did that.

Salomé: But he is not now, he is dead now, they are not listening now.

Claudia: But those pieces are part of our history, they are part of our soundscape. They are not like something that has happened then and now. *St Matthew's Passion* when it was written meant something completely different then, than when Mendelssohn conducted it or when we are listening to it now. So, it can be potentially even more relevant than any piece of music written or installed now.

Salomé: But it is also choking up the money and the space and the time for contemporary composition and contemporary sound works.

Claudia: Yes, I grant you that, but that doesn't translate into the idea that the music isn't relevant now.

Salomé: So the interpretation makes it relevant. So why not just for a year make this experiment of just listening to contemporary music. I would be very curious as to what would happen.

Thomas: You are trying to make a very clear line between what is dead and what is alive.

Peter Cusack: You mean we should stop listening to John Cage immediately?

Salomé: Yes, I actually think he is a good case in point, because I do think he overshadows a lot.

Peter: Yes I agree.

Salomé: I do think he stops a lot of what could happen.

Seth: Is there a related class argument, is that what you are making here?

Salomé: Yes, that is probably in there too.

Robert: It keeps going back to tradition, because people keep referring to classical music, and that finished with Beethoven. You're talking about tradition all the time. You are saying let's not listen to this music that has this tradition. Classical music was finished at the beginning of the 19th century.

Volkmar Klien: Why does our music always turn into 'classical' music? It does not exist in real life. Funding problems aside, but it does not exist in real life, it's the smallest part – why do we not talk about sound art versus Take That or some other big pop act. That would make for a more interesting discussion. Classical music does not refer to classical music as in music but as concepts that have been piled up on it.

Simon: It's called contemporary classical. But can I pick up on Seth's point about the concealed classism here. I think it is profoundly true, at least in British society, I don't think it is as true in Germany and other countries on the European continent, but it's profoundly true here. And I've always argued, and have bored people with it, that the problem is the distinction between an elite and a minority interest. The way forward is to create an ecological model, and you must preserve minorities. It's vital or the seed corn will be killed off in one season if something goes wrong. Minorities are the stuff of reinvention. But I have no problem in describing myself as a minority. If I start describing myself as an heir of Beethoven it's a disaster, clearly now, in the 21st century. And therefore the heir-of-Beethoven issue is over, the avant-garde said 'We're out in front, the rest will follow'. No it's not true, minorities yes, elites no. I mean elite in that sense that classical music has said for 150 years that it is an elite and that the rest is not valid.

Seth: It's a very familiar argument but this is a very particular elite.

Simon: Correct, I should not go against all elites. Shall we say privilege, then.

Nye: We can take Harrison Birtwistle who says there is nothing wrong with elites as long as anyone can join them.

Simon: Yes.

Nye: He's a case in point, he acquired most of his early musical background in a brass band in Manchester, which does not represent a class elite, and is writing what for a lot of people is very difficult, and very elitist music. Looking at it from a classical-music perspective, the people in conservatoires are very concerned by the fact that they lack relevance, and quite often you get the argument there that this is due to a lack of musical education amongst the rest of the populace. When you look at funding cuts in music education they have a point. Those of us who listen to Beethoven learned the piano when we were six or seven, quite a lot of us, not everybody, some people discover it later in life. But the more you get educated to that kind of music the more relevant it becomes. The relevance does not just come from its reflection of society, it comes from how you interpret society and what you see around you in relation to the work that you experience, and the musical work that you experience. Beethoven can still be relevant to our society if you have the tools to appreciate that. But we are kind of closing off that relevance through education cuts. That would be the argument in the conservatoires, and I think that is a perfectly legitimate point of view. I'm not saying that your point of view has no merit, because it has is in terms of being composers. I went to the 'Welt Ethos' of Jonathan Harvey the other day, and it seemed incredibly naïve. It was that typical thing that you get a lot in contemporary classical music, of closing yourself off from the realities of the world and make something that will form world peace through a C-major chord.

Justin: Can I just put forward a slight paradigm shift into a populist model, because it seems like a lot of metaphoric speak in this conversation has this sort of top-down attitude: soap opera, funding cuts, education. This might sound naïve perhaps as well but I think there is still room for vitality. I don't know whether we should make the presumption of the odds against good music to rise to the top because of funding cuts, lack of education. There could be an argument made for vital music, a vitality, whether it be in a sound/music tradition or a sound art tradition. A vital music that rises to the top, and engaged and demanding listeners, who are going to the galleries expecting a good experience, or crafting themselves a good experience. I think there is a bit of a tenor here that people are sheep, and are only looking at a painting for forty seconds, and I know for myself, and a lot of my colleagues and people I know, who are critical and demanding and engaged and who will gravitate towards things that are vital.

Angus: Nobody has mentioned what is good sound art and what is bad sound art.

Peter: Everyone is speaking as if sound art is just one thing, and it's all the same and clearly it is not.

Max Eastley: Technology changed the way sound art could be done in a gallery. If you wanted continuous sound you either had to do it kinetically, with a machine of some kind, or you would have a tape loop that ran round the gallery. But now you just have the digital thing, and you run a loop. Sound art with loudspeakers seems to be what people use mostly, loudspeakers and playback technology, and the loop is usually tailored, maybe in a lot of cases it is at most ten minutes, not four hours. You can enter it and leave it. It does not develop into anything else.

Simon: In your works Max do you have a concept of beginning and ending or is it just something you expect the listener to construct?

Max: Well it depends where you are in the gallery. They switch on and off. So you come in you see one which is not moving so you walk past it, and then you go and look at another and all of a sudden that one starts to move. It is an interesting thing between music and… I'm not absolutely sure whether it's music. Hans Keller once said you can't have music without a performer.

Stephen: In which case, is a recording sound art? It's an object, it doesn't change.

Max: Actually sound recording does change – I think if you play a piece of music that you really like to someone who is not going to like it and you are terribly enthusiastic, it actually changes while you are listening to it. I have experienced it so many times from the age of about fourteen, I put a record on and said 'Listen to this' and the person was going 'It's horrible'.

Stephen: But in itself it's an object, it does not change, and we assume, I mean most of us assume, that it's a performance. But it's not, it's an object.

Angus: Sometimes it might be a performance. It does not have to be an object.

Stephen: It might have been a performance but *it* isn't one.

Angus: It might be a 'sound art' performance, you can have a performance of sound art.

Stephen: Ah sound art, yes, but I was asking where does it all start, does it actually start with the recording of sound, and turning sound into an object, without us ever realising that what we are creating is an object which we can interpret as music, or not, depending on, as you say, whether we like it or not.

Max: Yes, we can deal with the disembodied sound of an orchestra, but if you think of the early sound recording of things, it's 'I wish we could see the orchestra'.

Salomé: Peter, can I quickly ask you what you meant by we don't talk about good and bad sound art.

Peter: I said you are talking about sound art as if it was all one thing. I did not mention good or bad.

Salomé: Oh sorry, so why did you say we do talk about sound art as if it was one thing?

Peter: For me, from a listening point of view, the big distinction is not between music and sound art, it's what you could crudely call the difference between abstract and figurative, in very visual art terms. I put most of music on the abstract side and sound art can fall either side. It seems to me, one of the processes of listening is whether you switch into an abstract form of listening, which music encourages you to do, and quite a lot of sound art too, or you want to get the narratives and identification and the actual sounds, which other forms of sound art encourage you to do; that to me is the interesting split. How we point our listening in different directions according to what we are asked to listen to. For me the distinction between music and sound art is relatively unimportant.

Thomas: The idea that performing a beat together is abstract, I mean it is certainly not representing anything, but it is a very profound experience in terms of the group.

Peter: I'm not saying one or other is more or less profound or meaningful or useful. I'm just saying there is that difference. The other thing that I would like to comment on: when Volkmar was speaking earlier he listed all the attributes of music. I thought yes, that's right, most of those I agreed with. And I referred back to my own experience as somebody who came through music to get to sound art and now I actually do a lot of stuff that I don't think is art at all, whatever kind of art. And I have to say it's been a very conscious and difficult process to rid myself of some of the ingrained reflexes of being a musician, and that is a very practical thing. For example, if you are a musician and are recording music you put your microphone in one place and leave it there. If you want to record the environment, it could well be better to pick your microphone up and walk around with it, but that is a very non-musical thing to do. Also with editing, usually you end up with far too much stuff and you have to edit. By what criteria do you decide that that is a good bit and that is the bit you are going to discard? Well all my criteria originally were musical ones, even if the sound in question had nothing to do with music, and it has been a very conscious process trying to first recognise these limits to my own listening, and then trying to combat them and change it. That has taken forty years and I still haven't finished. So, I like the idea of what Volkmar was saying, because I think music is incredibly insidious, and therefore I question Salomé, why you want to bring this into sound art. I think we are much better off without it.

Nye: I would like to know though Peter, why do you think that moving the microphone is not a musical thing to do. Did you not actually make a decision that it sounded better to use a moving microphone than a stationary microphone and were thus extending the musicality of your recording technique by doing this?

Peter: I am saying that if you record music, i.e. instrumental play, in a studio you find the sweet spot of any one instrument and leave the mic there, and before I recorded environments I did a lot of music recording. So my first techniques of recording were all those learnt in a music studio; I had to unlearn a lot of them to make it work somewhere else.

Nye: But there is maybe an undercurrent in how we are using the word 'music'. First of all, as Volkmar says, I don't think we can equate every group that creates music with the conservatoire. Music that is taught in conservatoires is this strange, eccentric subset of music that has developed in Western culture due to notation, essentially. Also are we not restricting ourselves if we are talking about music as this thing that is a habit – it's my habit to put the microphone there and record the guitar, there is no reason musically why I should do it. It might possibly be more musical not to. That decision you have made to rid yourself of habit is a very useful decision from your creative perspective, but ridding yourself of habit is not ridding yourself of music.

Peter: I don't think you learn anything without creating habits, otherwise you do not learn it.

Nye: Right, it is changing your habits then.

Peter: Yes, so what we are arguing about is what name to give to one, music or sound art.

Nye: And maybe that is the thing we should be arguing about sitting here in a colloquium on sound art and music. It is quite clear from our discussions ten minutes ago that people are using the word 'sound art' in very different ways, this afternoon particularly, and people are using the word 'music' in very different ways too, and we are jumping around these two terms as if we all agreed on what they are.

Stephen: Isn't Peter talking about musical tradition, not any particular music, but a way of behaving in a certain tradition and overcoming that pattern of behaviour, not classical, not anything, but just something that certain ways of music do to you when you learn it.

Cathy: I think Peter is just talking about his own habitual patterns.

Stephen: But I can identify with this.

David: We are talking a lot about the past. Leigh has raised the point, and Justin also, there is a real blurring going on here, and in all areas, and we are in a very dynamic situation. I can think of one good example: there is a massive worldwide hit record at the moment, which comes from Korea, *Gangnam Style*, that's interesting in itself because it is highly unusual for this country to accept a foreign-language record. Someone sent me a clip recently where they had taken out all the music and replaced it with environmental sound that corresponded to the video. They left in the vocals but all the music was filtered out. So if you see a horse you get horse sounds. One of the successes of this record comes from the video, which is highly entertaining. You get that feeling that we are on shifting ground at the moment, we are in a very dynamic situation, so fretting about Beethoven is not really the point.

Cathy: It really isn't the point, and I think we are all rather missing the point as well, and one of the points we are missing, is that we are the elite, well we are not exactly the elite maybe, but we are those people that we are discussing and criticising: we have representatives from the conservatoires, and a lot of people here are teaching. The minute we mention the word 'music' and mention it in opposition to 'sound art', we are setting up the new Beethoven-type canons. Of course we need Beethoven to be there somewhere in people's consciousness, but we do not need only Beethoven, in the same way that we don't need only sound art to be music that you encounter by walking into the work, and it doesn't have a beginning and end. Actually I think we've had a bit of a failure of imagination this afternoon.

Claudia: I think that's a negative way of thinking about it, because Nye just said we all have different ways of thinking about music and sound art. I think it's a perfect example of why we are coming towards your plurality. Isn't it marvellous that each of us has a different way of defining music, of defining sound art and thinking about it and yet we are all sitting together debating it which means that we are kind of getting there, I think. Because if we had a consensus that would really shock me. It would be horrible.

Cathy: Yes that is really good, but I guess my objection goes straight back into Salomé's book: if we're all thinking of something different, why are we using the same words?

Claudia: Well, because if we used different words for everything we could not even begin to have a debate.

Cathy: So those words on their own seem very reductionist.

Aura: But my understanding of this conversation, and I think it has been successful in some ways, we are certainly not here to define sound art or music, or even to establish a realm that could be close a category, but rather to explore what the tension between the two might provoke. I find some of the things that have come up in conversation very interesting and with much broader implications than just in relation to the little niche of sound art. Sound art is pretty niche, I mean music is everywhere, but sound art is very small, and maybe if you talk about the relevance of new classical music, for someone who is not interested in it, sound art is pretty irrelevant.

Cathy: Oh, I've never talked about the relevance of either of them.

Seth: To just pick up on them. Both music and sound art are two particular caves. As long as you remain in the cave you are always stuck, and you need a frame of reference that accounts for both, which is actually completely outside the scope of this debate. I betray my own interest here, but I think it has to be accounted for in terms of neurodynamics or other kinds of phenomena about what listening might be and how it may have evolved revolutionarily – I haven't heard any of those kinds of accounts of thinking about how does this stuff function? What does it do?

Thomas: Can I just, Allen, you have tried to say something several times.

Allen: Yes, can I say one quick thing? It's in relation to your talk, Thomas, and about your sense, which I take literally, of shifting ground. I was thinking of the two models you propose and it came up in many discussions, of the reciprocal and grounded mimesis. I think there is one point where they intersect and they become the same thing, and it is a domain of sound that everybody has skirted around but nobody has mentioned. By chance I was invited to the WFAE [World Federation of Acoustic Ecology] last year. And what struck me is that I think all of those people would have been thinking that the core of that discourse was left out today, because when one thinks about grounded mimesis, there is a part of grounded mimesis which happens in reciprocity, if one believes in deep ecology, which is to say that we are also in communication with certain aspects of the world, the animals and plants, that we are imitating. It seems as if that's a point where the two cross over and it is part of the shifting ground of a relatively new domain of sound art, it comes out of the soundscape movement. And it is curious that with the talk about mimesis and such it has not come up today.

Responses

Abstracts

Claudia Molitor

Composing for me is a process of listening, looking, and walking. A visual experience can be the starting point for a sonic idea, as can a touch sensation or a smell. Thus during the compositional process boundaries between senses are initially irrelevant and only become pertinent once these ideas approach a more concrete state. Some of my work is described (by others) as music, some as sound art, though in my mind whichever side of this apparent divide they fall into, they originate from the same artistic practice. By considering a recent work called *Vast White Stillness,* this response to the theme of the colloquium proposes an understanding of the terms 'sound art' and 'music' as invitations to the listener to inflect their approach *towards* rather than distinct definitions *of* a particular type of artwork.

Kathy Hinde

Three phone interviews with Kathy Hinde while she was recording pink-footed geese in the Montrose Basin in Scotland.

'I think the time spent out recording, and being immersed in that activity, is a good way to stimulate creative processes that are very open-ended. Although of course, on this occasion, I did have a specific purpose for a specific piece, and I have been mainly focussing on that, but ... other things happen during the process.'

First Response – Claudia Molitor

The Taste of the Apple: composing as process of listening, looking, drawing, and writing

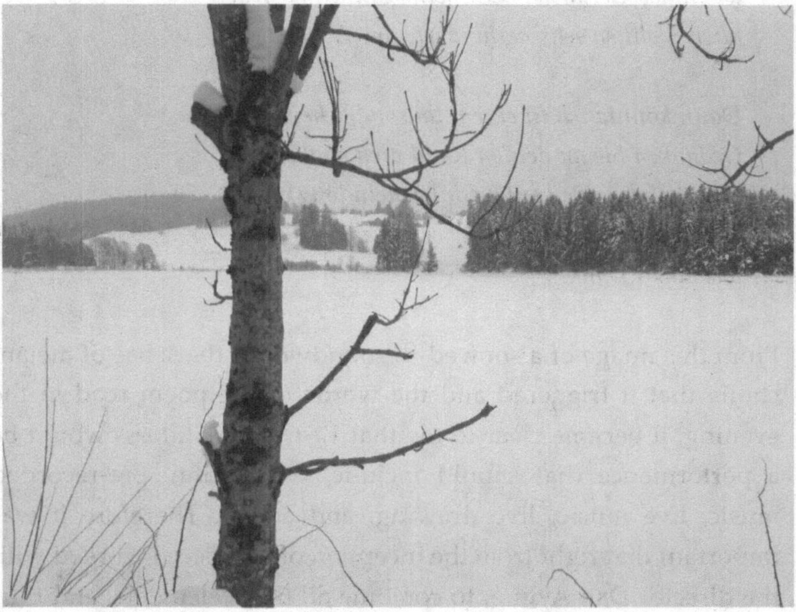

The photograph taken in the German Alps, which formed the starting point of the project

The starting point for my work *Vast White Stillness* (2014) was a walk in the Alps where I took an image of a tree in the wintry scenery and listened to the peculiarly still silence that befalls a landscape covered in snow. This particular soft sound of near silence, for me, allows internal thoughts and imagined sonic ideas to come to the surface. I find this both compositionally inspiring as well as intensely melancholic and at times disturbing.

That same evening I was reading a poem by Rainer Maria

Rilke:

Wenn es nur einmal so ganz stille wäre.
Wenn das Zufällige und Ungefähre
verstummte und das nachbarliche Lachen,
wenn das Geräusch, das meine Sinne machen,
mich nicht so sehr verhinderte am Wachen – :

Dann könnte ich in einem tausendfachen
Gedanken bis an deinen Rand dich denken
und dich besitzen (nur ein Lächeln lang),
um dich an alles Leben zu verschenken
wie einen Dank.[1]

From this image of a snowed-in soundworld, the sense of melancholia that it triggered and the words of the poem read in the evening, it became clear to me that *Vast White Stillness* would be a performance that should include image, film, pre-recorded music, live music, live drawing, and acting. Therefore it was important that right from the inception of the piece I worked with the director Dan Ayling, to combine all these elements, and thus *Vast White Stillness* is a collaborative work, created between him and myself and to some extent also the designer Rhiannon Newman Brown, who started working with us once our ideas had formulated into something a little more concrete.

The image above is the photograph of the tree in its snowed-in landscape, the still soundworld, that triggered the conception of the piece, and was slide-projected during the performance, appeared in the films, and formed the basis of the live drawings done by the actor. At the same time some of the field recordings made in this landscape formed part of the compositional material which was played back into the performance space via loudspeakers, a record player, a piano, and a music box.

For me music touches us so deeply and emotionally because it not only resounds in space and in us, as three-dimensional beings; it also embodies the experience of the passing of time. In the same way that light illuminates space, sound also seems to illuminate temporality. It makes us acutely aware of the flow of time and our entanglement in this flow. In this way it brings us close to our mortality and yet highlights our present aliveness, as our listening to it captivates our sense(s) in the present.

When I say *music*, what I really mean to say is 'my listening to', and this 'listening to' could be to what we might term music or sound art or simply noisy stuff. It is in fact 'my listening to' which I believe *frames* the heard as music.[2]

Here I would like to propose, in relation to the theme of this colloquium, that this moment of framing, or listening to, is prejudiced by culturally constructed distinctions between music and sound art that direct the way we approach any instance of sound-based artwork. And it is these pre-established ideas that in turn colour and set up our listening even before a single vibration has filled the atmosphere to en- and in-velop us. In other words our listening *to*, is always already inflicted, prejudiced, or educated with frames that determine how we understand the heard: either as music or sound art or noisy stuff.

There are many modes of listening that are culturally determined and agreed upon from the outset of our hearing experience. While, as stated above, these will prejudice what we are about to hear, they also make it possible to have a communal framing, a shared 'listening to', indeed a collectively agreed 'music' or 'sound art'. This collective agreement is what Juhani Pallasmaa in his book *The Thinking Hand* alludes to when he talks about existential space in art and architecture as being produced by individual and collective experiences and memories, but it is equally relevant for sound:

> Existential space is structured on the basis of meanings and values reflected upon by an individual or group, either

> consciously or unconsciously; existential space is a unique experience interpreted through the memory and experience of the individual. On the other hand, groups, or even nations, share certain characteristics of existential space that constitute their collective identities and sense of togetherness. The experiential lived space, not physical or mathematical space, is the object and context of both the making and the experiencing of art and architecture. (Pallasmaa 2009, p. 128)

Our perception of sonic space (music, sound art, or the sounding environment) is, just like Pallasmaa's existential space, understood through individual and collective experiences that mix or collide with normative social and cultural influences and historic prejudice. It is the framing of our 'listening to', laden with our experiences, pre-conceptions and expectations (both individual and communal) that turn the work that is encountered into a piece of music, a sound art work or something altogether different. The intentions of the artist, composer, or improviser can come into this too, and play a part in the process of framing, but it is the 'user' (if I may use this word) of art, in this case the listener, who continues to change the way any piece of music or art is conceptualised, understood, and read. To quote Ola Stockfeld (2005): 'each genre also has a number of genre-normative modes of listening, and even these have changed over time in relation to […] choices of strategies of the listener.' Furthermore, when we listen to music, sound art, or our environment, we are experiencing our encounter with the 'listened to'. Therefore, should we really ask whether something is music or sound art, or is the question of why and how something resonates as music or as sound art with a listener not far more relevant?

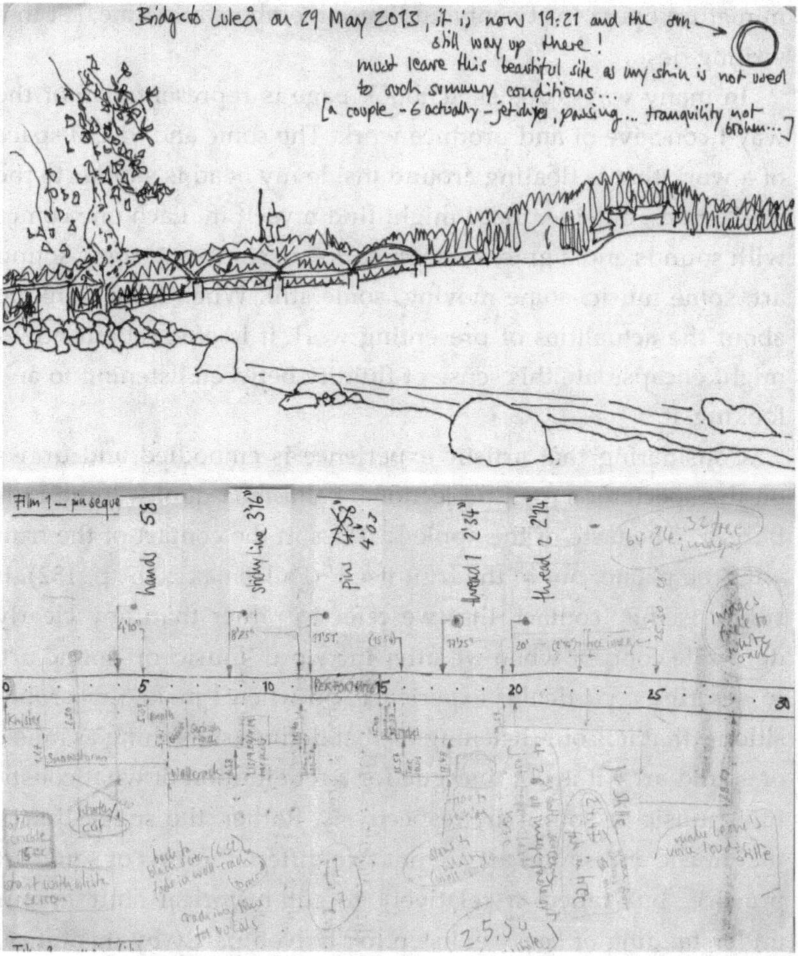

An early sketch for a possible performance sequence

On the bottom half of this image is a possible temporal mapping of the songs, the field recordings, the films, and the performance interventions. Although this is not how *Vast White Stillness* eventually unfolds during performance, this represents the first plan of how the diverse material might sit together in a performance situation. At the top is a drawing from a beach in Sweden where I was performing *Remember Me...* a forty-five-minute miniature opera for twenty audience members at a time, set in a writing desk.

In many ways, this sketchbook page is representative of the way I conceive of and produce work. The sonic and visual space of a work that is floating around inside my head is similar to the 'real' space, outside, that I might find myself in. Each one comes with sounds and sights, some intentional, some not, some sound art, some music, some moving, some still. When I am thinking about the actualities of presenting work it is often about how I might encapsulate this sense of fluidity between listening to and looking at.

Considering that artistic experience is embodied and draws on the spectator's own projections, Pallasmaa quotes Jorge Luis Borges: 'The taste of the apple [...] lies in the contact of the fruit with the palate, not in the fruit itself' (Pallasmaa 2009, p. 132). It surely is this 'contact' that we refer to rather than any clearly definable concept when we utter the word 'music' or 'sound art' to describe a particular experience. So when I make my proposition – that it is our 'listening to' that defines something as music or sound art – it is not to argue for a redefinition of what constitutes music or sound art respectively. Rather, the suggestion is that music and sound art are not two different forms of sonic-art practice, but reflect a relatively recent historical shift in our understanding of *how* we 'listen to'. Driven partly by theoretical and philosophical shifts in ideas around perception, discussed by thinkers such as Maurice Merleau-Ponty, Jean-Luc Nancy, or the anthropologist Tim Ingold, but also by technological possibilities of sound recording, editing and reproduction. This to me suggests that the naming of an artistic practice or a body of work as 'sound art' or 'music' might be understood as a signal to the listeners: a signal that encourages or even directs them to alter the way they listen to a given piece of sounding art, rather than saying anything in particular about the work in itself.

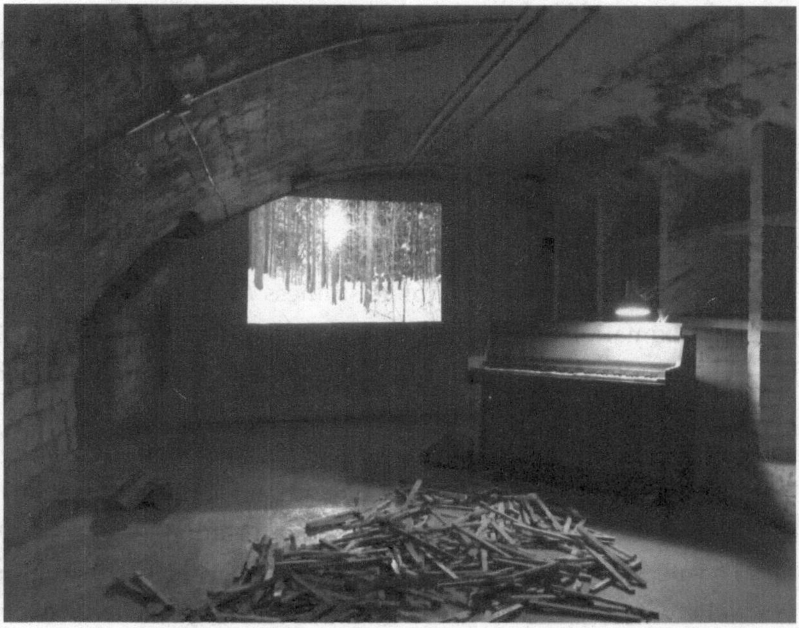

One of the spaces *Vast White Stillness* was performed in during Brighton Festival 2015

Bibliography

Ingold, Tim. 2000. *The Perception of the Environment: Essays on Livelihood, Dwelling and Skill*. London and New York: Routledge.

Merleau-Ponty, Maurice. 2004. *The World of Perception* (1948). London and New York: Routledge.

Nancy, Jean-Luc. 2007. *Listening*. New York: Fordham University Press.

Pallasmaa, Juhani. 2009. *The Thinking Hand: Existential and Embodied Wisdom in Architecture*. Chichester: Wiley Publications.

Rilke, Rainer Maria. 2006. 'Wenn es nur einmal so ganz stille wäre' from 'Das Buch vom Mönchischen Leben' (1899) in *Rainer Maria Rilke: Die Gedichte*. Frankfurt am Main and

Leipzig: Insel Verlag.
Stockfeld, Ola. 2005. 'Adequate Modes of Listening' in Cox & Warner (eds.), *Audio Cultures: Readings in Modern Music*. New York and London: Continuum International Publishing Group.

Notes

1 'If for once there was complete stillness / If happenstance and approximations / fell silent as well as neighbourly laughter / if this sound that my senses make / wouldn't keep me so much from waking // Then I could envelop you / within a thousand-fold thought / and possess you (just for the length of a smile) / in order to gift you to live, / like a thanks' (From 'Das Buch vom Mönchischen Leben' 1899, own translation).

2 The use of the word 'framing' rather than 'constructing' is deliberate here as our listening does not so much construct something from bits of heard material, but rather has the ability to frame the heard in a variety of ways. A simple example is the sound of a distant motorway. I may simply ignore it and focus on the foreground sound; I may be intensely irritated by the constant hum, thus shifting it to the foreground of my attention; or I may imagine it to be a raging river in the distance, thus drastically re-framing what this sound might mean to me.

Second Response – Kathy Hinde

Three Phone Conversations in the Field: recording pink-footed geese in the Montrose Basin in Scotland

[Dial tone. Phone ringing.]

Kathy Hinde: Hello?

Salomé Voegelin: Hi Kathy, this is Salomé.

Kathy: Hi, how are you?

Salomé: I am well thank you, how are you? I'm really happy you have agreed to do these phone conversations while you're in the field. It's really exciting that I can catch you as you are recording pink-footed geese in the Montrose Basin in Scotland. Can you tell me where that is exactly?

Kathy: It's in-between Aberdeen and Dundee.

Salomé: Is it very cold?

Kathy: Yes it is quite cold, I thought it would be colder but it's still quite cold when you're outside standing still.

Salomé: Have you done any recordings this morning?

Kathy: Yes and I also made one recording last night, well, in the afternoon, when I arrived.

Salomé: How does the recording of pink-footed geese in the

Montrose Basin in Scotland relate to your practice as a musician, sound and visual artist?

Kathy: My work is often inspired by the natural world and frequently by birds, by their behaviour, their migratory routes, or their song. I make work that frequently fuses visual art and sonic art. To answer your question I am going to describe what I experienced this morning with the geese and how I observed that visually and sonically.

Firstly just to say I am recording the geese specifically to use with my installation *Piano Migrations*, which is going to be shown in Aberdeen in a couple of weeks' time. I wanted to make the work site-specific to the location where the piece is being shown, and this area is really famous for the pink-footed geese wintering here. There have been 70,000 or more on Montrose Basin in the autumn, there are less here now. I am filming the geese specifically for *Piano Migrations*, because this installation maps bird flightpaths into sound by sensing where they are flying and turning that into a player-piano. But I am also here because I like to find opportunities for recording and filming birds because I find it very inspiring for my practice as a whole.

So this morning when I went to see the geese. I got there before it was light. I arrived in the dark, I had already thought of a good spot to go to. I set myself up firstly with my camera, video camera, and I had sound recording gear as well. And what's amazing is that it was dark, I could not really see where they were and I saw dark patches on the surface of the water that could have been geese or that could have been ducks or other birds. I was gradually getting used to the dark and having a look around and then a whole flock of them took off. The first thing is hearing them: you hear this distant calling that builds in volume and then you can sense where they are coming from and from the darkness you can see some movement, and as they reach higher in the sky you can see them forming their distinctive V shape.

And that is when I started trying to film them.

What is amazing visually about them taking off is that they take off in a huge cloud, and they are all overlapping and it fills the screen of my viewfinder, which becomes a constantly shifting but full frame of geese. And I can pan back and then gradually as they take off and spread out you sometimes see this really distinctive V shape and sometimes you see them forming an almost perfectly straight line, and they can just in a moment dissolve into what looks like a completely random configuration again, and that is really wonderful for the purpose that I am filming them for because I use these images to play a piano, using all these different visual configurations of how the geese are flying; but it is also wonderful just in terms of thinking of ideas and being inspired by the behaviour of the geese. This forming into lines and V shapes, and the shifting into what feels like a random configuration to then form a different defined shape, I find really inspiring as a way of thinking about making work or constructing pieces and composing.

Also the sound of the geese, because they fly in flocks, you hear this constant sound of a flock of geese, it's a collective sound, it's one thing, but listening closer, you hear it is made up of all these individual geese calls, which are constantly changing and overlapping in different ways and that is incredibly dynamic, with lots of movements and shifting configurations. But then thinking about it as a whole it is one sound and I am fascinated by how you can make one compositional piece or an audio-visual piece that is a very distinctive thing but also within that one thing it has a kind of indeterminate shifting behaviour that is generative, that constantly changes; so if you observe it at a different scale you can find these different levels. And so thinking about listening to and watching the geese on those terms it relates to how I make works that are audio-visual. For instance the piece I am making for *Piano Migrations* uses birds to play the piano and it is a very distinctive piece. This installation uses an old, broken piano from which I have removed the keys and hammers to reveal the strings and soundboard. This 'piano-harp' is then hung up on a metal frame and I project a video of birds directly onto the piano strings and soundboard. I then worked with a software programmer to create a system that means, wherever the birds fly, they trigger a small motor or tapper to play the piano string in that location. The broken piano becomes a mechanically controlled acoustic instrument that is activated by videos of birds. The overall impression is that the birds are flying past the piano and their wings are touching the strings to create a percussive, prepared piano piece.

So in that sense it is very easy to describe it as a sculptural sonic piece, but when I use different videos of birds to play the piano I do not know what it is going to sound like until I use that video and play it on the piano, and so for me I have created a framework which is the system I have put in place using this piano with a video-tracking system that always changes depending on where the birds fly on the videos. Also, I use different pianos and I prepare them in different ways so that changes the work all the time. And so as a single piece it is quite recognisable but the actual precise nature of the sonic and visual events are completely down to where the birds fly and what angle I film them from and their behaviours and speed of flight and the way that the patterns that they create shift and change.

There is something quite inspiring about the act of going out into the wild and recording the geese. There is something about the amount of time that I wait for them, to find out where they are, or waiting for them to take off or discovering how they behave in the morning at that particular place at that time of year, which is always different each day. But just to spend some time out here on my own observing, there is a sort of spaciousness and a space for thought and also for really close observation. You get really drawn into where the next flock is going to take off and you are really listening hard, you are looking in great detail. And in terms of spending a few days doing that this is a really good process for thinking creatively, and a good space.

Salomé: It is really great to listen to you, because as you talk, I'm thinking this is what is missing in the discourse on field-recording, the idea that field-recording is a human pursuit: these geese are there whether you are there or not, but it is how you interact with them and how you make sense of them and how you make sense of yourself within the field by being there and being in relation to the geese, and so what is missing in the discourse on field-recording is the focus, on authorship, on the field-recordist, where they are and how they relate to the field.

What is the weather like where you are?

Kathy: This morning it could not have been a more perfect day for going out to record the geese, it was a really, really clear sky, and even though I arrived an hour before the sun rose you could already see some light in the sky, and very few clouds, and it was very expansive because the sky just felt really huge.

I guess one really defining factor was that it was incredibly windy, which of course makes it really difficult to record sound and also quite difficult to film because it pushes you over all the time. Really, really windy, even though the basin is quite sheltered, I am on this little bit jutting out into the basin. It is not actually the coastline, it's slightly inland.

The light was amazing and as the sun rose it was incredibly bright on the surface of the water. But yes incredibly windy and after two hours of standing virtually in the same place it was also incredibly cold. So I had to come indoors for a little bit, and I am going out again in about an hour.

Salomé: And you are there by yourself, in a house?

Kathy: I am staying in a B&B and it's actually a wonderful place, it's quite close to Montrose Basin but it is just in the middle of nowhere and it's absolutely gorgeous, it has amazing views. I also saw some geese on my way back but they spread out for the whole day. They go over the fields and feed and so they could be anywhere in the region and then they come back to the Montrose Basin at the end of their feeding day to sleep.

Yes I am here on my own. It is now actually not as windy anymore, and it's really, really sunny, it is still cold but it's not windy.

Salomé: Ok, I will ring you again tomorrow at twelve o'clock.

Kathy: Sure, that is perfect.

Salomé: Great, wonderful, and so good to talk to you.

Kathy: You too and thanks for ringing.

Salomé: Bye!

Kathy: Bye!

*

[Dial tone.]

Salomé: Hi Kathy, this is Salomé.

Kathy: Hi, how are you?

Salomé: So, can you tell me a bit what the weather was like today and what you did today?

Kathy: Sure yes, the weather was a lot calmer, it was not as windy and not as cold, it was very still but quite cloudy so it was not as bright, that is how it was. I got there when it was really dark and I accidentally scared away the geese by not realising they were really close to me.

Salomé: What time of the morning do you set out?

Kathy: I go out just before six o'clock, sunrise at the moment here is at eight-twenty, but it always starts to get light about an hour before sunrise, and they call it first light. A lot of birders talk about first light, because it's when the birds wake up and they start taking off, but actually, where I am going on the Montrose Basin the sky looks enormous, you can almost see the curve of the earth, and it starts to get light earlier than that, it starts to get light at about quarter to seven or even six-thirty. So I try to get there before that happens.

I went out to the place I have been going out to, and it was really dark, and I did not have a torch with me, because I didn't want to disturb the geese or any other wildlife. I had two cameras and two tripods with me which is quite a lot of stuff, and I realised I could hear the geese and they must be really close but I could not see where they were and I just very carefully crept over this slight hillock of grass and they were really close to the shore of the basin but because I came over this little hillock without realising where they were, they all flew off. So that was a bit of a disaster, they all flew off. I mean it was amazing actually, it wasn't a disaster but it was really dark so I did not see them I only heard them and I did not record them. I just did not realise that just me creeping around in the dark they would actually sense me, but they must have done.

Salomé: Yes, They are probably attuned to every movement and every smell that's different.

Kathy: Exactly, so to start with I was really excited that I could hear them and that they must be close, because it is a huge place this basin so they could be anywhere, and I was really excited that I might be really close to them, and then of course I was really close to them and they flew away [laughs].

I did get to experience that. Then I think they went to settle again at the other side of the basin.

Salomé: But it brings to the point, that the field recordist will change the field.

Kathy: Yes, absolutely, and also – thinking about this – one of the weird things that always happens – if you are waiting for something, like waiting for a flock of geese to take off, for maybe an hour or something like that – watching closely – as soon as you think this is not going to happen and you put away your recording gear and your camera… it happens. Guaranteed.

Salomé: In our phone conversation yesterday you talked about 'the whole thing and the many parts' and you were referring to the geese, their flight formations and shifting behaviours as flocks. Can you talk a little bit about how you relate or translate the whole and the parts of the natural world that you are recording into the whole and the many parts of your work?

Kathy: I was thinking about that and I looked into how geese fly in formation. And they do it so they can save energy and they help each other by flying in this V formation. It has to do with how the vortexes of the air flow, and they have to beat their wings out of phase with the bird in front at a particular distance behind that bird and then they can fly really smoothly and it is as if the first bird is carving a pathway through the air and all the other birds follow exactly the same pathway in the flow with their wings. They take it in turns to do that so they all work together to save energy so they can do their long migration routes.

Also, thinking about the way that swarms and flocks of animals, particularly birds and many other species, work in groups like that, I also really like going to watch the starlings performing their murmurations, which happens quite close to where I live in the south-west of England. So observing that and learning about that, each bird is part of the flock, the flock is the whole thing and each bird is a single part of that flock and follows an instinctive range of behaviours. With the geese it is about being just out of phase with the bird in front so their flying is easier and I guess they would learn that through experience and realising that a certain way of flying makes things easier. And then with the starlings perhaps they are grouping together to make themselves look like one big organism, so they are not as vulnerable to predators, but also the way that they move, each bird needs to stay about the same speed as the bird next to it and avoid obstacles. So with all the birds in a flock, if every bird does that, that's three simple rules, I am sure there are more, but if we take three simple behaviours: fly the same speed, keep the same distance from the surrounding birds, and avoid obstacles, then as a whole thing this produces complex patterns, because as one bird might get into an eddy of wind that moves it slightly, or there is a predator and they need to move out of the way, then this ripple, this one slight movement of one bird, can spread across the flock just through each bird working in relation to the bird next to it and you get these really complex patterns. And so thinking about that and bird flocking and the whole thing and the many parts, I am really interested how that can relate to how you might work with something like an open score, in music-making. You might have a score that has got a set of simple instructions that each performer follows, and you can have many, many performers, and through that you can create complex music. I am really interested in that.

Also because I work quite a bit with technology and I work

with a computer programmer, I am thinking about how you can model behaviours using computer algorithms where you can give many parts very simple instructions that might work on a small element of randomness that then creates this really intricate complex behaviour that is one whole thing. And I am interested in the whole thing also having a certain quality, or aesthetic, or a way of being described as one thing and the reason that it exists is that these many parts do many very simple things. So yes I am interested in looking at things in this way, and to give an example of a piece that I have made that most relates to this way of thinking is a piece called *Vocal Migrations*. It is inspired by how bats echolocate and how they use sound to see. And it is also a bit inspired by and a nod towards Alvin Lucier's piece *Vespers*, where people use these clicking 'Sondols' to find their way in a room by listening to sonic reflections. I wanted to make a piece for people to use their voice to navigate without using their eyes. I just wanted them to listen to their own voice. Again I worked with a programmer and some technologists and we built a little wearable device that means that you can sample your own voice and then the device will adjust the way that the vocal sample plays back depending on how close you are to other things. It currently exists as an installation constructed as a paper labyrinth, so each person taking part goes into the labyrinth blindfolded by this device and they make their own vocal calls and listen to how this device then treats their vocal call, and they can navigate through this labyrinth by listening to how their own voice is changed. My thinking was to send a lot of people into this labyrinth and what emerges is a kind of music based on these vocal calls and their abstraction through the technology. And so giving people a simple task, I like to call it a behaviour, many vocalists go into this labyrinth and create a complex overlapping vocal score that has a certain quality to it that is recognisable as that piece but is always changing depending on who is in there and what they are doing.

Salomé: So you are using tasks and formations in a way as a conceptual trigger to do things, like what the flock of birds does, or to enable people to perform something that creates particular behaviours and patterns?

Kathy: Yes I think so, it is kind of the idea of describing the behaviour rather than a specific outcome. Describing a behaviour that could produce a complex group.

Salomé: Is it like there is indeterminacy but there is also extreme control?

Kathy: Yes.

Salomé: What you are feeding in, the rules, or the parameters of the behaviour, always create a whole despite everybody doing something distinct. It creates a whole and determines how it remains collective.

Kathy: Yes.

Salomé: The reason I asked this question about the one thing and the whole, is that I read back through the transcript of the colloquium and the issue of the whole and the parts came up a lot in relation to music and sound art. The whole work, how it is created, the beginning middle and end was widely discussed but I felt that in the conversations of the colloquium these issues still remained quite abstract, and it struck me in our conversation yesterday that how you are dealing with this in your work is very hands-on, as a score, as a graphic score, as parameters of composition. So your answer brings another interpretation to this question of the musical piece as a whole that is very applied and brings a different criticality to it.

What are you going to do with the rest of the day?

Kathy: Unfortunately while I am here I do have some work that I really have to finish, so I am going to stay in and do that. But I am going back out again hopefully at two o'clock, to see what I can find. Because this morning I was filming the geese for a little bit but there weren't that many and then after I had done that I went to walk around a completely different part of the basin just to explore different spots, because I had noticed right on the other side there were lots of waders that were too far away to see, and then they all flew off. So I hope that when I go back out this afternoon I will be more lucky. It looks like it's going to be really windy again.

And I am going to see the visitor centre. There is a nature-reserve visitor centre.

Salomé: Are there other people where you are at this time?

Kathy: When I go out in the afternoon I always meet someone, I never meet anyone in the morning, but I always meet someone in the afternoon. So on the first day there were two older guys that had come to see the geese and they were into birding. And then yesterday there was a guy taking photographs because the tide was out and there were lots of really amazing reflections.

But it is interesting because everybody has got something to say about where you should go around the Montrose Basin, with intricate descriptions of little paths you can go down, so I went off to find a few of those this morning.

Salomé: Wonderful, thank you, have a great rest of the day and looking forward to speaking to you again tomorrow.

Kathy: I do too, bye

Salomé: Bye

*

[Dial tone.]

Kathy: Hello?

Salomé: Hi Kathy, this is Salomé.

Kathy: Hi, how are you?

Salomé: How are you today, this is your last day today, so how did it go?

Kathy: Well when I went out this morning there was some kind of storm happening.

Salomé: Yes, it's really windy here too.

Kathy: When I went to go out it was really, really windy and it was raining, sort of horizontal sleet, and so I decided to wait until later. Just because I thought, well I would...

I should really have gone but it was pretty extreme.

But it is kind of extraordinary because I am out now, and the weather has completely changed, it is still really windy, but it is a completely clear sky with really bright sunshine and the tide is out on the Montrose Basin and all the mud is shining and reflecting in the sunlight. It has completely changed, and I have noticed in Scotland the weather can change in an instant. Apparently it is snowing not that far away.

Salomé: It must rain, or must have a lot of snow and rain in Scotland.

Kathy: Yes it does, although each time I have been to the east coast, sort of Dundee and actually Montrose, it's been really bright sunshine.

Salomé: I really enjoyed our conversation yesterday, particularly in relation to formations and how you compose with them. I found it really fascinating. And when I listened back to the recording I thought what else do I want to know? I had lots of more questions which I tried to condense into one with a few sub-questions, so let me start with the main question: You seem to respond to, and mimic or interpret the behaviours of the geese you are recording, the individual smaller movements and the larger movements they produce in a very conceptual way using it to score, organise sounds and images, or even to conduct the movements of the performer/audience member.

From here I would like to ask what is the status of listening in your field-recording process and in your final artwork?

Another related question is: Does what you hear influence how you experience and thus use the flight formations? What I mean by this is, are you bringing a musical hearing to the geese's behaviour? This relates to how much we can or not switch off what is almost maybe a professional disability, a professional tendency, where you hear already formations in a musical and aesthetic way?

Kathy: First of all I want to say I am in a bird hide, I am out in the middle of the basin but I am in a wooden box with flaps to open so you can see out. Basically it is really, really windy here so I am right in the middle of the basin completely on my own but I have come into this wooden box on stilts, really high up which they put out for people to watch birds from. You do not disturb the birds so much and it is sheltered. But I do not normally go in them because you can't look up, they just have these flaps that you can look out of, and you can see all the way round but you cannot spin around and look up into the sky.

You get this strange tunnel of a wooden staircase and brass-plated door handles. You are in the middle of this amazing landscape in this strange homemade box. There are folders and people write down birds they have seen, and there is a massive pair of binoculars, which you can use. It's really nice because there is a lot of trust.

I wanted to point out where I am, in response to your question about the place of listening.

I am aware that I have spoken a lot about the visual aspects of the geese and what it inspires me to do, the kind of patterns and formations. I have not recorded much sound while I am here but listening has been just as much a part of being here and being in this environment. Listening to the sounds of the crowds of geese gives me a sense of scale and of where they are and their level of activity and the dynamic. And I also hear other birds: there are oystercatchers and curlews. I haven't spent much time listening to oystercatchers before, and on the first day there were two oystercatchers doing a kind of amazing duet, which I listened to but did not record. But it has made me really aware of the sound of oystercatchers in this environment amongst all the... mainly the sound of the wind and when the tide is in the sound of the faint lapping of the water. So, I have been very aware of the sounds while I have been here. To come close to your question, when I am field-recording without a necessary, specific piece or purpose in mind, I would probably be doing sound and photography and film, and I just want to comment on the difference between those briefly. Is that useful?

Salomé: Yes certainly.

Kathy: So when I am recording, you know, my experience of field recording and sound and filming, when I am recording sound, I need to be doing one at the time really, it is a bit difficult to do both, I learnt that the hard way, you always mess them both up. When I am trying to capture something or I record something in sound, most of the decision-making process takes place at the beginning really: where I position myself, where I position the microphone, the direction of the wind, because that can make things quite difficult to record, what levels, where I am in the proximity to various things. All that sort of decision-making and thinking happens at the beginning and then I just sit extremely still and listen, because I cannot move as it will make a sound and I do not usually want my own movements to interfere with those kind of recordings, which relates to what you pointed out a few days ago, that a field recordist changes the field. So then the actual process of the recording becomes a completely intensely focused and still listening experience that is magnified by the fact that I am using a microphone, and that's quite meditative. Although I am kind of semi thinking about the technicality of the recording and watching the levels, making sure the wind is not distorting it, and things like that, it becomes a very still and meditative activity.

Whereas having tried to film birds, I also need to do preparation before I start, where I am, what lens I am using, and all this kind of stuff, but the actual activity of filming the geese involves a lot of decision-making in the moment about how to frame this particular event visually in the camera; how to move the camera; where to follow. It feels like there is a little bit more intervention in how I am capturing the geese visually. But also it demands a different state of mind, because there is a lot of thinking about technique and camerawork required. Even though I am really focused on looking and observing there is a slightly different frame of mind to be in. So yes, just thinking about the differences between those processes for me, and about your comment on how what I hear and see influences how I perceive and experience the flight formations and how I might use the footage, the only way I can think of answering this for you is that when I am watching the geese I am looking through the camera and I am noticing the things that I was talking about the other day, about the phasing of their wings and how they follow a pathway one after the other, and then I kind of automatically think about how this is a bit like sine waves, how they go out of synch and how they might cause interference. Those sorts of things go through my mind. It's not necessarily related to what I am hearing but it is related to what I am seeing. But also, this formation that goes from being in a straight line or a V shape into something that is overlapping, chaotic, and random makes me think about dynamics, textures, rates of change, compositional shapes, and how that might relate to sound. I gain inspiration from the geese, when I am listening to them, and because I am listening to them in a flock, I am thinking about the textures and the dynamics of that and the shapes of it and what that suggests. I guess the ideas that grow out of listening to them and watching them manifest themselves in sound and as visual ideas.

Salomé: The way you describe it now it sounds like you are bringing a musical or sonic sensibility to your seeing them, the geese. It is almost like a simultaneity, that at the same time as you are seeing them, the way you are seeing them the way you think about them suggests a sonic appreciation of their movement and what they look like. Do you think that is right?

Kathy: Yes I think that is true. I have never thought about it or articulated in that way before but I think I do. I think it has a lot to do with the fact that I am always trying to make work that is a balance between the sound and the visual, and that they depend on each other and one is not privileged over the other. But I think also in the past I have done a lot of visuals for live-performance music, dance theatre, work in a live context, so I am always thinking about gathering imagery that I feel suggests a kind of musicality or a textural rhythm or a compositional shape, and so I am sure that I approach filming things with that mindset instinctively.

Salomé: And do you think it is more a musical hearing, do you bring in your musical training and ideas of scores, or is it a sonic hearing, freed from conventional expectations of musicality, or is it both?

Kathy: I think it is both and I think that's because more recently I have been doing more sound recording in the field and it has really heightened my awareness to the sounds around us, but I still often think about them musically, possibly, but it's tricky to know…

Salomé: But maybe there is not such distinction. Or maybe the question is whether it is a purposive listening: you already know you want to make a piece from it or is it more about the sound you hear?

Kathy: I don't think I always go as far as thinking about what the piece might be, but I become more aware of the things I am drawn to and the things I might want to gather and might want to use, what I might want to work within a piece. For example, when I think of the oystercatchers it has really stayed in my mind, these two high-pitched rhythms that go in and out of synch and their changing speeds and rates, and I am thinking that might be an amazing pattern and structure to model or shape in a composition. But, also, these thoughts coexist with lots of other things, and then at some point, they may feed into a piece, sometimes perhaps in a small way, or even subconsciously. I think the time spent out recording, and being immersed in that activity, is a good way to stimulate creative processes that are very open-ended. Although of course, on this occasion, I did have a specific purpose for a specific piece, and I have been mainly focussing on that, but… other things happen during the process.

Salomé: In relation to this, when you think of your audience – and yesterday you said that in some of your work, your audience becomes a participant that is being moved through formations as well. So are they a listening audience, do you want to get them into the work through the sound, or is for you the sound and the visual completely equivalent?

Kathy: It does vary but in that particular piece, *Vocal Migrations*, where the audience becomes immersed inside the work, and they kind of make the piece, it is very much about listening and about the sound that they are making. But when I introduce them to that process and I frame it with the idea that bats use sounds to see, it starts to have a conceptual angle as well, so that yes, it is very much about them being immersed in the piece and listening.

But the other piece that I spoke about, *Piano Migrations*, in that piece I do not want to privilege either the visual or the sound. I would like to think that they have an equal status in the piece although it is completely up to how someone perceives it, but I think the sound on its own is not interesting enough, and the projection of birds onto piano strings without there being any reaction or response does not really make any sense, and it is the two together that make the piece what it is and they are completely dependent on each other.

One of the things I am after with my work is to bring the audience into an immersive, experiential piece. Of course I am working with concepts and ideas as well, but the initial engagement I want the audience to have is quite experiential and not over-intellectual. In that way trying to create something quite immersive can be very effective. I hope that bringing people into an immersive environment heightens their sense of listening or observation. And so I think as my work progresses, I'm discovering that sound has a great capacity to create an immersive space, because it's not, or it does not have to be, you know, you don't necessarily need to be anywhere particular within that space and within the sound to experience it. Whereas with the visual, with objects, or sculptures, or projections, you are looking at it, you are placed more deliberately and it is maybe not as immersive, although I don't want to reject this as a possibility, as light too can be very immersive.

A recent piece I have made is called *Tipping Point*, and it is to do with using water levels to change sounds. I started with an idea, with a concept again, which is to do with shifting water levels and the water cycle and our relationship with water, trying to highlight some of the ecological issues relating to water resources. I approached the actual piece very much starting with sound and I think in the finished piece the sound is the thing that draws people in, but then the sculptural visual aspect of the work comes to peoples' attention and I hope they develop a fascination with what is happening and what is making the sound and the concepts and meaning behind the piece. But then again this is a piece that people walk right into the middle of, and it's kind of all around and so… it is still a bit of both.

The desire to try to create an immersive space through my artwork relates also to the desire to share the experience of being out in the wild, field recording, filming, or simply walking, watching, and listening. Taking time to observe and appreciate the world around us. Within all the work I create, there are environmental concerns woven in. I don't highlight issues explicitly, but my aim is to try and share an appreciation of the natural world and the importance of taking care of the environment.

Salomé: A question that comes out of your work for me is: how do these things meet between listening and watching? Where does the emphasis lie, because somebody who goes into the field as a sound recordist only has a much easier time. The recordings can remain unresolved, in process.

Kathy: Yes, I think that may also be true, which relates to what I was just saying about how sound might remain more open to audience interpretation in a finished work than the visual aspects.

The balance between listening and watching is one of those things that is constantly shifting in my work. Definitively, in the last year or so I have tried to shift my practice and process more towards sound because of what I was just describing of wanting to create an immersive space for the listener.

But I also find sound interesting in terms of your question about the audience. There are a few other pieces I have made that are online as sound maps. You can play the map as a score and listen online. But actually, the sound map is an invitation for other people to make recordings and put them on the map. The maps are themed: one is about birdsong, and another one maps Aeolian sounds made by the wind, and yet another one is more workshop-based. For this last one, I go out with people and we make recordings of their local area and then decide what we are going to put on the map, the sounds we think are important or we like best, or perhaps that feel the most musical. So with that one the most important part is the people actually experiencing recording sound and listening to what they are recording through microphones, to kind of share the process of field-recording which enlivens how you might appreciate the sounds around you in general. -

So, in some ways, these sound maps and listening walks are a way to invite people to listen more closely, by using a microphone – and hopefully the follow-on effect is that one will continue to listen more closely in everyday life, and be more fascinated with everyday sound.

Salomé: What is the website for that work?

Kathy: The birdsong map is called twitchr.co.uk, so it is spelt wrong, without an e. And the soundwalks one that is based around workshops is echo-location.org.uk. The Aeolian one was connected to a group show with Max Eastley, http://aeolian-soundmap.co.uk.

I think these sound maps are more about the process of making them. The birdsong sound map is a pet project because I made it and I use it as a bit of an excuse to organise bird-recording walks with an expert. I get an ornithologist involved and we go for a walk and invite people to join us. We do not necessarily always make a recording, we kind of watch and listen and the ornithologists will talk a bit about birdsong or whatever their specialist area is.

The thing about this work is going on these walks, that is the key thing. It brings people together to listen and observe and be engaged with birds and birdsong, and each other. It brings a lot of people and experiences together. And then there is the online instant-upload aspect of the piece with people who like recordings and other people can find these recordings online and have a listen too.

I am working on a new one that maps hidden underwater courses in Glasgow, it is called *Submerge,* it will be an installation, and the website for the process is here: www.submerged sounds.co.uk. For this work I went out with people to follow and trace the streams that run through the city, and record them. It was partly about finding and walking these natural watercourses through the city together, to trace them, find them, observe where they plunge underground into culverted pipes, and re-discover the points where they reappear… And it is also partly about listening to the hidden underwater sound worlds… and of course, these two things are connected in the sense that both are highlighting the usually invisible, ignored, and inaudible aspects of a particular place.

With this in mind I can answer your second initial question about professional tendency, where you hear the field always already in a musical and aesthetic way. I wonder if, when I listen in a more intense way, I do bring a kind of 'musical' listening to the field? I don't know if this necessarily relates to my musical training, or whether it is more like a searching for an immersive place, or a way of being in the world that is more connected via the senses rather than through intellect or the decoding of information. I expect the two relate, and the intensive listening in the field affects my compositional skills, or musical performing skills, as they are to do with close, detailed listening.

There is a comparison with the act of making music, or performing, in that you aim for a very focused state where the attention to detail is heightened. So... perhaps there is a connection with the fact that close listening is enhanced through field recording, and because of my musical training I bring musical listening to my field recording?

My comment about musical training also relates to some of the live performance work I'm currently exploring, which is performing with instruments or sound sculptures that I have built myself. So far, these constructions tend to present an anti-virtuosic 'interface', in that some aspects of its control are not exact, or definitely predictable. I create quite open scores for myself to follow, but the performance is always partly improvised. The fact that these 'instruments' have their own behaviours, and I can't predict exactly how they will respond, means I am in dialogue with the instrument, by improvising and responding to it. For me, this brings another level of immersion to my experience of performing, and perhaps a more heightened sense of listening.

Salomé: Listening to you talking about listening has made me much more aware of my own environment and immersion here in my living room, the gurgling fish tank, the hum of cars driving past, and the buzz of the fridge, and how they might form a dialogue, a composition or performance. To finish can you also give me the links to the other pieces you have mentioned in our conversations?

Kathy: Sure, the other pieces I have referenced in the conversation are:

Piano Migrations – http://kathyhinde.co.uk/piano-migrations-installation/ – I haven't posted a page on the Aberdeen pink-footed geese version yet. I will try and get that on my website and send you a link. And here are also the links to *Vocal Migrations* and *Tipping Point* which I mentioned too:

Vocal Migrations – http://kathyhinde.co.uk/vocal-migrations/

Tipping Point – http://kathyhinde.co.uk/tipping-point/

Of course – I need to find the photo of me in the bird hide and the windy recording of what it sounded like inside…

Salomé: Great, thank you so much, it's been really inspiring talking to you. Have a great time recording the geese still.

Kathy: Bye!

Salomé: Bye!

Postscript – Kate Lacey

Reading the Colloquium: undisciplined reflections

It is an interesting prospect (by which I mean flattering, intriguing, daunting...) to be asked to reflect on a debate about a critical framework to renegotiate the borderland between music and sound art, when professing no particular expertise in either field. My own work treats listening as a civic practice in an age of media, and engages, on the face of it, with very different concerns. It certainly begins from very different disciplinary traditions – history, communications, politics – that themselves traverse yet another set of borders, between the humanities and the social sciences. In preparing this response, I have been very conscious of my role as eavesdropper on a debate whose intellectual hinterland is for me quite alien terrain, and whose contours might become distorted as I filter them through a foreign disciplinary lens. Despite the clarity and vivacity of the discussions represented in this volume, there is always a danger, then, that the comments that follow might misconstrue, or even miss the point entirely – for all that the broad new school of 'sound' might be gathering us together in a new conversation. These misgivings notwithstanding, if there is a virtue in offering a perspective as someone who is neither familiar with nor invested in the debate, it must surely be the possibility of casting these inter- and intra-disciplinary discussions in a different light, or perhaps I should say transposing them to a different key. In that spirit, this response does not aspire to offer an overview, or even a critical review; it simply offers some of the ways in which the debate has resonated across one particular disciplinary divide, and I hope that it will also echo in some measure the format of the whole collection in offering something of a provocation.

Certainly, for the uninitiated, it comes as something of a

surprise to discover this 'rift' between music and sound art, which seem from the outside to have rather evident elective affinities. In particular, it was surprising to learn that sound art might have closer affinities with the world and discourse of visual arts than it does with the musical, and that music is not necessarily something that is audible. In grappling with these ideas, it did make me speculate about the convoluted, and at times paradoxical, interplay between the abstract and the material in the development of these apparent distinctions (the complex institutional, philosophical, and technological histories notwithstanding). In other words, if sound art has emerged from the visual arts, and if it has been shaped by the same moves towards abstraction and conceptual art, then might that be the same as to say that it moves away from the visual to the musical, which was (always?) already perhaps the most 'abstract' of the arts? Similarly, as the visual arts aspire to and encroach on that more conceptual territory, perhaps the materiality of music begins to come to the fore as a marker of distinction?

Whatever the background story of the rift, the desire to confront and overcome this divide – to work towards a shared analytical framework and a common critical language – is presented in Salomé Voegelin's opening statement, and it seems to have been an important part of the original motivation for her and Thomas Gardner putting together the whole event. Acting as both invitation and provocation, Voegelin's essay does not form the opening contribution of this collection, which seemed, on first reading, a rather odd editorial decision. Instead, proceedings are opened by Allen S. Weiss' essay on the 'democratisation' of the Japanese tea ceremony, a subject matter that might seem unduly specialised for a broad-ranging discussion on form and method in the sounding arts. And yet, as the collection unfolds, it becomes apparent that the themes encapsulated in this short sketch, like the ceremony it describes, echo as some sort of leitmotiv through the whole book. Here we find a sonic practice carefully traced out in the interplay between the material and the ideational, but also a melancholy tale of loss (of depth, authenticity, exclusivity, understanding, integrity), which underlies a more optimistic narrative of new ways of listening enabled by new encounters. The once exclusive and encrypted sounds of the tea ceremony, when opened to the ears of new classes, generations, and nations, find new resonances and associations with other traditions, leading to new knowledge and new practices, but also to a newly contextualised understanding of the 'original' form. These then, in miniature, are the contradictions – the threats and promises – inherent in the process of opening up a practice, of making public. Disciplinary boundaries offer security, community, specialisation, coherence. These are significant values, not to be lightly dismissed. But they bring with them the dangers of isolationism, self-referentiality, obscurity, and atrophy. Dancing the disciplinary divides in a way that preserves the integrity of tradition while being open to the revivifying challenges of contestation is an art in itself.

Some of the insecurities and jealousies of the various tribes represented in the debate between music and sound art become evident in the course of the discussions – the sound artist envious of the funding, status, and concert halls of the classical musicians; the classical musician bemoaning the marginalisation of their art; the electro-acoustic artist dreaming of inclusion as a sound artist in the Turner Prize shortlist; the musicologist hoping for a less rigid curriculum. It is probably true to say that an entirely harmonious and consensual public sphere can only operate under conditions of already-existing equality of resources, shared forms of cultural capital, and agreed legitimations. So it is perhaps not surprising, given the different constituencies of the participants and the traditions they represent, that for all the talk of breaking down boundaries, the round-table discussions revealed there is still a lot at stake in defining terms and territories and markers of distinction – even within what, from the outside, might seem to be a relatively cohesive field.

While recognising that this internecine rivalry might be precisely the space where innovation takes place or is inspired, in truth, these are all minority sports, albeit enjoying varying degrees of cultural cachet. At one level, there is a dizzying array of sonic practices and musical forms referred to in these discussions – concrete poetry, field recording, performance art, installations, experimental and classical music, to name just a few – and the biographies of the contributors reveal many stories of experimentation and artistic 'border-crossing'. And yet amidst all this diversity, there is notably little mention of most popular musical genres (in both senses of the word, either folk or commercial). With some notable exceptions, these are referenced, if at all, as if in parentheses – perhaps because they already complicate the notion of a dualism between music and sound art. But I also picked up on several interventions that seemed – problematically, from my cultural-studies perspective – to strain against the popular as standing for the distracting, the effortless, the seductive, even the dangerous. Such language reveals a troubling perpetuation of the classical and hierarchical divide between the pure and the barbarous, between sensory perception and critical reflection, between passivity and agency, albeit that the conversation also turned to sonic practices that explicitly set out to overcome such boundaries, as in Aura Satz's discussion with Thomas Gardner on the immersive qualities of perception and the dissolution of the boundary between self and other.

Similarly, many of the contributors join Voegelin in making impassioned calls for an analytical model that would break down, circumvent, or otherwise simply ignore restrictive definitions and disciplinary divides. On the whole, these incline to a certain idealism, playing with words like, 'utopia', 'Elysium', 'groundlessness', 'dreamworlds', or an 'open space', where everything is always possible and, implicitly, equally valued.

Such visions, however, do tend to sideline institutional and sociological questions of power and politics. One such is Simon Emmerson's vision of a networked ecosystem of minorities without elites, where the 'bio-diversity' of the sounding continuum with all its generative potential could be preserved. It is a seductive vision, but hard to see what kinds of practical strategies could serve to overcome existing or emerging differentials in power and prestige.

Cathy Lane, too, argues eloquently for difference, resistance, and change. She rails against definitions and boundaries, at least as far as a neat dualism goes. She would prefer to see in its stead a messy pluralism, where 'works' (a label she uses deliberately to highlight the effort that goes into making a piece and how it demands effort in return) are 'judged on their own terms', and not on the terms of the market or the academy. Perhaps this phrase is transparent to practitioners of the creative arts, but from the outside, it is not clear if these 'terms of judgement' might be aesthetic, political, ethical, experiential, cognitive – or any, all or none of these. More to the point, it is not clear how such a radical diffusion and proliferation of criteria – as many as there are works, by the sound of it – could be sustained, nor what would be at stake in the judgements that are made, if not to set up new borders between works that succeed and those that don't, according to the terms of the day?

From a rather different perspective, Volkmar Klien, too, declares himself against definitions in art on the grounds that 'all attempts to normatively define specific art forms have proven to be futile, utterly impossible and [...] obstructive'. He calls for musical composition to be a truly 'open-ended process' that can go even beyond the sonic; nonetheless he can still argue against 'organised sound' as a synonym for music on the grounds that such a term ought also to include (spoken) language. Certainly the terms are not synonymous, but presumably it could be the case that music, sound art and the spoken word are all sub-sets of 'organised sound', which would imply that it is the boundaries within, not between, that are at stake, and where precisely one might expect to find these boundaries overlapping, porous, mutable, or indistinct.

More than one contributor mentioned how sound art is perhaps more aware of or bound by its context than classical or electro-acoustic music. And yet it seems to me that each of these has an audience and connections beyond their immediate aficionados in a way that sound art – particularly gallery-based sound art – does not, or at least not yet. Perhaps another way of conceiving this is the sense that I get from this discussion that some sound artists retain – or seek to retain – more control over the conception, conditions, reception, and interpretation of the work; a control that is inevitably relinquished with the passage of time, and the disembedding from particular locales and audiences that comes with reproducibility, be that via performance, publication, or technological mediation. Certainly you see this in Lane's demand for works to be judged on their own terms, and even more stridently in Voegelin's provocative refusal to play the compositions of those who have died, as if the meaning and relevance of a composition were the sole property of its author, unanchored in any living tradition, be it musical, theoretical, cultural, or technological. Driven, as it seems to be, by a (playful?) desire for funding to be redirected towards the production of new works, rather than the reproduction of old ones, such a proposal could, moreover, be seen to fit very neatly within the current neoliberal frame, in privileging individual expression disconnected from a sense of communion (with the past, as much as with others in the present), mistaking the current moment as being necessarily new, and packaging that novelty for a marketplace, whether commercial, artistic, or academic, where novelty for itself is highly valued.

Perhaps that is to overstate the case – and I should say that a counterargument about the resistance of contemporary sound art to commodification and the pursuit of a shallow novelty could be made – but it's a reading that comes from my having been sensitive to a persistent focus on authorship throughout the collection, for all the contestations around nomenclature (composer, artist, or practitioner). This is a focus that seems to chime, knowingly or otherwise, with a prevailing politics of voice where self-expression is taken to be an end in itself, and is certainly privileged over the politics of reception and communication in the fully interactive sense of the word. This privileging of authorship connects, necessarily, with another predominant focus through the collection: the centrality of the text or the work, and its performance or realisation.

Nye Parry usefully traces the debates between music as symbolic code revealed in performance, and music as realised in the moment. At the risk of oversimplifying what is clearly a complex and nuanced historiographical and philosophical field of enquiry, the crux of these debates seems to rest in the search for *the* meaning of music. This is a kind of critical enquiry that is really quite alien to someone schooled in the field of media and cultural studies, where meaning is generally understood to exist in a mobile field of tension between the moments of production, text, and consumption, and to be dependent on any number of contextual variables. Certainly, as an 'outsider' to these debates on music and sound art, one of the striking consistencies across the various positions represented here is the centrality of the text, whether that is conceived as work, score, or performance.

Parry's own conclusions demonstrate how much these debates about the meaning of a text have centred on and been driven by notions of power/knowledge and control across debates in and around both music and sound art; that is to say, the authority and authenticity of the author might also belie a certain authoritarian desire in those forms of authorship that seek control or ownership of some sort over sounds and listeners. The listener and their listening are consistently conceptualised as being, in effect, *produced* in relation to the characteristics of the (always-authored) text, even where the listener is involved as co-producer.

Having written a book on the idea of 'listening publics' (where 'listening' is taken to be a civic disposition and 'listening out' is presented as an ethical responsibility in contrast to the 'listening in' to specific texts, be they media or musical), my contribution to the debate, then, would be to ask what happens if there were to be a radical shift to centre on the listener? Not the listener as interpellated or defined by the work of art, but the listener who pre-exists the text and even the imagination of the author? There is some sense of this in Simon Emmerson's invocation of the listener's expectations, although this is framed more as an injunction to the composer to help the listener embark on auditory paths less trodden. And there is certainly something of this sort at work in Claudia Molitor's discussion of conceptualising the practice of listening 'towards' a work of art. It certainly rings true that the expectations, education, competences, and intentions that a listener brings to a piece will frame that listener's naming of the piece as either music or sound art (or not), but this naming is not entirely wilful, as it must stand in relation to the terms already in circulation.

In the very first discussion, picking up on Weiss' introductory essay, Parry points out the contradiction that the very practice of listening to the materiality of sound in the moment – the kind of listening practised by tourists ignorant (or innocent?) of the complex history and theory of the ceremony – is something very close to the kind of 'different' listening advocated by Voegelin. However, he is careful to acknowledge that this is a historically specific listening, possible only in the wake of 20th-century theorisations of sound and music. But this qualification seems to me still to restrict this kind of listening to a specific cognoscenti – albeit one now schooled in a modernist Western musicological tradition, rather than that of the ancient East. This acquisition of specialist musicological knowledge, or training of the ear, is surely just one of the aspects of historical specificity at work in shaping the kinds of listening that listeners are able to bring to a sound event. The international tourists listening to the Japanese tea ceremony stand in metymonically for all accidental encounters with the sounding arts. They may or may not know how to decode the sounds appropriate to the formalities of either tradition, but they will almost certainly be bringing to the encounter an auditory capital hugely extended, and arguably enriched, by the ready availability of and access to (via mobility and mediation) a vast range of sounds and music. That these ears have not been trained in a specific tradition does not mean that they are entirely untrained in making sense of sounds disembedded from their immediate (unmediated) cultural context and origin.

Here my own interest in the relationship between listening and media technologies becomes apparent. There was certainly much to recognise in the contributions about how both disciplinary debates and compositional practice change in response to changing technologies, but I would just observe that from my perspective there seem to be a couple of blindspots within the discussion. The first is the apparent equation, broadly speaking, of technology with recording or computing technologies, as if the gamut of musical instruments and other sound-making devices were not also forms of technology, not to mention the historical variety of inscription devices used in producing scores. The second is the relative lack of attention in the debates to the technologies of mediation and their effects on the production, distribution, and consumption of all forms of organised sound. Again, I am conscious that this might well be an unfair criticism, with these issues simply lost in translation between our different idioms. But certainly as a radio scholar I was struck by the almost deafening silence about the consequences for this discussion of considering a medium which either in practice or in principle might not only enable audiences to hear and engage with sound-works defined as either music or sound art, but that might precisely schedule a programme designed to blur or question, or sustain and reinforce those boundaries at least, to use a quaint old BBC phrase, 'at the listening end'.

There are so many important aspects of the colloquium that I have not commented on, though not for want of interest. But I want to end with a brief reflection on the creative format of the book, made up as it is of provocations, responses, dialogues, debates, and then this final reflection. There are many conference proceedings which get written up in much more conventional ways – with papers simply turned into chapters following a thematic introduction from the editors. Here, the intricate structure produces a sense of a debate unfolding, of participants circling around ideas, of ground being tested, divides being bridged, and differences being celebrated. Certainly, the decision to transcribe the discussions, rather than to summarise them, lends these sections a peculiarly sonic quality, as the voiced interactions of live debates leap off the page. And I've already suggested not only that Weiss' overture acts as a palimpsest of the debate as a whole, but that it sets up the leitmotivs that recur in different guises throughout the whole; and it strikes me, as I write this coda, that the whole collection has a musical sensibility, with its different movements, its call-and-response form, its interplay of theory and practice, its polyphonic stylisation, and its striving for harmony among the dissonant voices – albeit a striving that has not yet found its resolution.

Biographies

Simon Emmerson is Professor of Music, Technology, and Innovation at De Montfort University, Leicester. Recent commissions from Bourges, Paris, and Berlin festivals. Recordings of his works are available from Sargasso. Previous writings include *The Language of Electroacoustic Music* (Macmillan, 1986), *Music, Electronic Media and Culture* (Ashgate, 2000), and *Living Electronic Music* (Ashgate, 2007). He was founder Secretary of EMAS (The Electroacoustic Music Association of Great Britain) in 1979 and on its board till 2004, and a trustee of its successor organisation 'Sound and Music' 2008–2013. In 2009–2010 he was DAAD Edgar Varese Visiting Professor at the TU, Berlin.

Thomas Gardner is a composer, improviser, teacher, computer programmer, and academic. His work is concerned with the relations between sound art and music, focusing on group interaction and the kinds of change introduced by electronic media. His practice consists of composition, improvisation, the design of instruments and software, and the exploration of new performance contexts. Recent works have been performed at the Sibelius Academy, Dartington Festival, Institute of Contemporary Arts (ICA) in London, Alte-Schmiede Vienna, and the Salla Chavez in Mexico City. He is course leader of the MA in Sound Arts at the London College of Communication.

Kathy Hinde's work grows from a partnership between nature and technology expressed through audio-visual installations and performances that combine sound, sculpture, image, and light. Drawing on inspiration from behaviours and phenomena found in the natural world, she creates work that is generative; that evolves; that can be different each time it is experienced. Hinde frequently collaborates with other practitioners and often involves the audience in the creative process. She has shown work across Europe, Scandinavia, China, Pakistan, USA, Colombia, and Brazil. She is an Associate Artist with Art Production House, Cryptic, in Glasgow, Scotland. In 2015, Hinde received an Honorary Mention at Prix Ars Electronica for her installation *Tipping Point*.

Volkmar Klien grew up in Vienna, spending his childhood engulfed in the city's rich musical life with all its glorious traditions and engrained rituals. Working from this background Klien today strives to extend traditional practices of composing, producing, and listening far beyond the established settings of concert music. He works in various areas of the audible and occasionally inaudible arts navigating the manifold links in-between the different modes of human perception, the spheres of presentation, and the roles these play in the communal generation of meaning. He is a Professor for Composition at the Anton Bruckner University in Linz. www.volkmarklien.com.

Kate Lacey is Professor of Media History and Theory in the School of Media, Film, and Music at the University of Sussex. She has published widely on broadcasting history and the question of how emergent media forms are bound up in the formation of publics, and is the author of *Feminine Frequencies: Gender, German Radio and the Public Sphere 1923 to 1945* (University of Michigan Press, 1996) and *Listening Publics: The Politics and Experience of Listening in the Media Age* (Polity, 2013). She was a founding member of the *Radio Studies Network* and *The Radio Journal: International Studies in Broadcast and Audio Media*, and sits on the UK Radio Archives Advisory Committee.

Leigh Landy holds a Research Chair at De Montfort University (Leicester, UK) where he directs the Music, Technology, and Innovation Research Centre. His scholarship is divided between creative and musicological work. His compositions include several for video, dance, and theatre and have been performed around the globe. His publications focus on the studies of electroacoustic music. He is editor of *Organised Sound* (CUP) and author of eight books. Most recently his ebook, *Compose Your Words,* was published (Intelligent Arts, 2014). He directs the ElectroAcoustic Resource Site (EARS) projects and is a founding director of the Electroacoustic Music Studies Network (EMS). www.mti.dmu.ac.uk/~llandy.

Cathy Lane is an artist and academic. Her work uses spoken word, field recordings, and archive material to explore aspects of our listening relationship with each other and the multiverse. She is currently focused on how sound relates to the past, our histories, our environment, and our collective and individual memories, from a feminist perspective. Cathy is Professor of Sound Arts and University of the Arts London and Co-Director of CRiSAP (Creative Research in Sound Arts Practice).

Claudia Molitor is a composer/artist whose work draws on traditions of music and sound art but also extends to video, performance, and fine-art practices. Exploring the relationships between listening and seeing as well as embracing collaboration as a compositional practice is central to this work. Her work is regularly commissioned, performed, and broadcast throughout Europe. Recent work includes *The Sonorama* with Electra Productions, Turner Contemporary, and the British Library, *Vast White Stillness* for Spitalfields Festival and Brighton Festival, and 2*TwoLO* for NMC's 'Objects of an Exhibition' project with the Science Museum. www.claudiamolitor.org.

Nye Parry has made sound installations for major museums including the National Maritime Museum, the Science Museum, and the British Museum, in addition to concert works and more than twenty contemporary-dance scores. As a research fellow at CRiSAP (2011–13) he developed the installations *The Exploded Sound* and *Significant Birds* which have been shown in Europe, the USA, and Asia. From 2003–2011 he was programme leader for the MA in Sonic Arts at Middlesex University. He has a PhD in Composition from City University and teaches at the Guildhall School of Music and Drama and Trinity Laban Conservatoire.

Aura Satz's practice encompasses film, sound, performance, and sculpture. Her projects engage with sound-visualisation technologies, as well as key female figures excluded from mainstream historical discourse in relation to electronic music, technology, science, and labour. She has performed, exhibited, and screened her work internationally in galleries and film festivals, including Tate Modern, Tate Britain, the Hayward Gallery, Barbican Art Gallery, ICA, the Wellcome Collection, BFI Southbank, Whitechapel Gallery (London); Gallery 44 (Toronto); Gertrude Contemporary (Melbourne); De Appel Art Centre (Amsterdam); and Baltic Centre for Contemporary Art (Gateshead). She is Moving Image Tutor at the Royal College of Art, London.

David Toop is a musician, author, professor, and Chair of Audio Culture and Improvisation at London College of Communication. He has published five books including *Ocean of Sound, Rap Attack,* and *Sinister Resonance*. Exhibitions curated include *Sonic Boom* for the Hayward Gallery and *Playing John Cage* for Arnolfini Bristol. His first album, *New and Rediscovered Musical Instruments,* was released on Brian Eno's Obscure label in 1975 and he has collaborated with artists ranging from John Latham, Bob Cobbing, Carlyle Reedy, and Ivor Cutler to Rie Nakajima, Evan Parker, Max Eastley, and Akio Suzuki. He has recently completed part one of *Into the Maelstrom: Music, Improvisation and the Dream of Freedom,* a two-volume work on free improvisation.

Salomé Voegelin is an artist and writer engaged in listening as a socio-political practice. She is the author of *Sonic Possible Worlds: Hearing the Continuum of Sound* (Bloomsbury, 2014) and *Listening to Noise and Silence: Towards a Philosophy of Sound Art* (Continuum, 2010). Her work brings the philosophy of sound to a participatory engagement: encouraging a sonic sensibility through public interactions, and pursuing through performance an uncurating of sound. Her collaborative practice, with David Mollin, establishes through words and sounds conversations and reconfigurations of relationships and realities. Voegelin is a Reader in Sound Arts at the London College of Communication, UAL. www.salomevoegelin.net.

Allen S. Weiss is the author and editor of over forty books on performance theory, landscape, gastronomy, sound art, and experimental theatre, including *Phantasmic Radio* and *Varieties of Audio Mimesis*. His radio work includes *Glissando* (a Hörspiel) and *Radio Gidayū* (a Kyoto soundscape) for Deutschlandradio Kultur. He directed *Theater of the Ears* (a play for electronic marionette and taped voice based on Valère Novarina) and *Danse Macabre* (a marionette theatre for the dolls of Michel Nedjar), and most recently *Poupées des ténèbres* (a documentary film on Nedjar's dolls). He teaches in the departments of Performance Studies and Cinema Studies at NYU.

Contemporary culture has eliminated both the concept of the public and the figure of the intellectual. Former public spaces – both physical and cultural – are now either derelict or colonized by advertising. A cretinous anti-intellectualism presides, cheerled by expensively educated hacks in the pay of multinational corporations who reassure their bored readers that there is no need to rouse themselves from their interpassive stupor. The informal censorship internalized and propagated by the cultural workers of late capitalism generates a banal conformity that the propaganda chiefs of Stalinism could only ever have dreamt of imposing. Zer0 Books knows that another kind of discourse – intellectual without being academic, popular without being populist – is not only possible: it is already flourishing, in the regions beyond the striplit malls of so-called mass media and the neurotically bureaucratic halls of the academy. Zer0 is committed to the idea of publishing as a making public of the intellectual. It is convinced that in the unthinking, blandly consensual culture in which we live, critical and engaged theoretical reflection is more important than ever before.

ZERO BOOKS

If this book has helped you to clarify an idea, solve a problem or extend your knowledge, you may like to read more titles from Zero Books. Recent bestsellers are:

Capitalist Realism Is there no alternative?
Mark Fisher
An analysis of the ways in which capitalism has presented itself as the only realistic political-economic system.
Paperback: November 27, 2009 978-1-84694-317-1 $14.95 £7.99.
eBook: July 1, 2012 978-1-78099-734-6 $9.99 £6.99.

The Wandering Who? A study of Jewish identity politics
Gilad Atzmon
An explosive unique crucial book tackling the issues of Jewish Identity Politics and ideology and their global influence.
Paperback: September 30, 2011 978-1-84694-875-6 $14.95 £8.99.
eBook: September 30, 2011 978-1-84694-876-3 $9.99 £6.99.

Clampdown Pop-cultural wars on class and gender
Rhian E. Jones
Class and gender in Britpop and after, and why 'chav' is a feminist issue.
Paperback: March 29, 2013 978-1-78099-708-7 $14.95 £9.99.
eBook: March 29, 2013 978-1-78099-707-0 $7.99 £4.99.

The Quadruple Object
Graham Harman
Uses a pack of playing cards to present Harman's metaphysical system of fourfold objects, including human access, Heidegger's indirect causation, panpsychism and ontography.
Paperback: July 29, 2011 978-1-84694-700-1 $16.95 £9.99.

Weird Realism Lovecraft and Philosophy
Graham Harman
As Hölderlin was to Martin Heidegger and Mallarmé to Jacques Derrida, so is H.P. Lovecraft to the Speculative Realist philosophers.
Paperback: September 28, 2012 978-1-78099-252-5 $24.95 £14.99.
eBook: September 28, 2012 978-1-78099-907-4 $9.99 £6.99.

Sweetening the Pill or How We Got Hooked on Hormonal Birth Control
Holly Grigg-Spall
Is it really true? Has contraception liberated or oppressed women?
Paperback: September 27, 2013 978-1-78099-607-3 $22.95 £12.99.
eBook: September 27, 2013 978-1-78099-608-0 $9.99 £6.99.

Why Are We The Good Guys? Reclaiming Your Mind From The Delusions Of Propaganda
David Cromwell
A provocative challenge to the standard ideology that Western power is a benevolent force in the world.
Paperback: September 28, 2012 978-1-78099-365-2 $26.95 £15.99.
eBook: September 28, 2012 978-1-78099-366-9 $9.99 £6.99.

The Truth about Art Reclaiming quality
Patrick Doorly
The book traces the multiple meanings of art to their various sources, and equips the reader to choose between them.
Paperback: August 30, 2013 978-1-78099-841-1 $32.95 £19.99.

Bells and Whistles More Speculative Realism
Graham Harman
In this diverse collection of sixteen essays, lectures, and interviews Graham Harman lucidly explains the principles of Speculative Realism, including his own object-oriented philosophy.

Paperback: November 29, 2013 978-1-78279-038-9 $26.95 £15.99.
eBook: November 29, 2013 978-1-78279-037-2 $9.99 £6.99.

Towards Speculative Realism: Essays and Lectures
Graham Harman
These writings chart Harman's rise from Chicago sportswriter to co founder of one of Europe's most promising philosophical movements: Speculative Realism.
Paperback: November 26, 2010 978-1-84694-394-2 $16.95 £9.99.
eBook: January 1, 1970 978-1-84694-603-5 $9.99 £6.99.

Meat Market Female flesh under capitalism
Laurie Penny
A feminist dissection of women's bodies as the fleshy fulcrum of capitalist cannibalism, whereby women are both consumers and consumed.
Paperback: April 29, 2011 978-1-84694-521-2 $12.95 £6.99.
eBook: May 21, 2012 978-1-84694-782-7 $9.99 £6.99.

Translating Anarchy The Anarchism of Occupy Wall Street
Mark Bray
An insider's account of the anarchists who ignited Occupy Wall Street.
Paperback: September 27, 2013 978-1-78279-126-3 $26.95 £15.99.
eBook: September 27, 2013 978-1-78279-125-6 $6.99 £4.99.

One Dimensional Woman
Nina Power
Exposes the dark heart of contemporary cultural life by examining pornography, consumer capitalism and the ideology of women's work.
Paperback: November 27, 2009 978-1-84694-241-9 $14.95 £7.99.
eBook: July 1, 2012 978-1-78099-737-7 $9.99 £6.99.

Dead Man Working
Carl Cederstrom, Peter Fleming
An analysis of the dead man working and the way in which capital is now colonizing life itself.
Paperback: May 25, 2012 978-1-78099-156-6 $14.95 £9.99.
eBook: June 27, 2012 978-1-78099-157-3 $9.99 £6.99.

Unpatriotic History of the Second World War
James Heartfield
The Second World War was not the Good War of legend. James Heartfield explains that both Allies and Axis powers fought for the same goals - territory, markets and natural resources.
Paperback: September 28, 2012 978-1-78099-378-2 $42.95 £23.99.
eBook: September 28, 2012 978-1-78099-379-9 $9.99 £6.99.

Find more titles at www.zero-books.net

www.ingramcontent.com/pod-product-compliance
Lightning Source LLC
LaVergne TN
LVHW040446111026
849885LV00037B/408